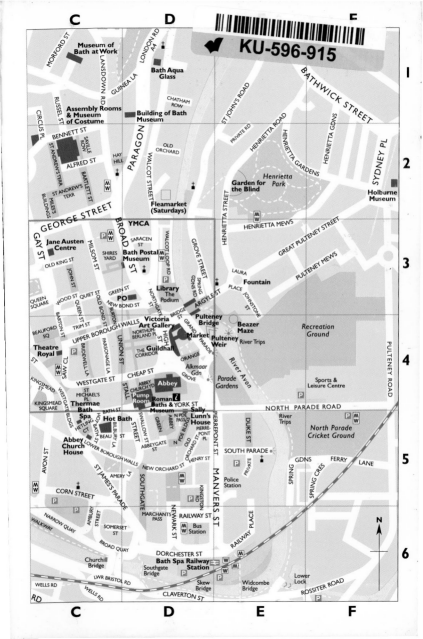

KU-596-915

C   **D**   **E**

MORFORD ST
Museum of
Bath at Work
LONDON RD
A4
Bath Aqua
Glass
LANSDOWN RD
GUINEA LA
CHATHAM
ROW
ST JOHN'S ROAD
BATHWICK STREET
1

Assembly Rooms
& Museum
of Costume
Building of Bath
Museum
PARAGON
OLD
ORCHARD
PRIVATE RD
HENRIETTA ROAD
HENRIETTA GARDENS
HENRIETTA GDNS
SYDNEY PL
RUSSEL ST
CIRCUS PL
BENNETT ST
SAVILLE
ROW
ST ANDREWS TERR
ALFRED ST
HAY HILL
WALCOT STREET
Henrietta
Park
Garden for
the Blind
Holburne
Museum
2
ST ANDREW'S
TERR
BARTLETT ST
MILES'S
BUILDINGS
M W
Fleamarket
(Saturdays)
HENRIETTA STREET
M W
HENRIETTA MEWS

GEORGE STREET
GAY ST
YMCA
BROAD ST
SARACEN
ST
WALCOT LOOP RD
GROVE STREET
GREAT PULTENEY STREET
PULTENEY MEWS
3
Jane Austen
Centre
Bath Postal
Museum
P M
SHIRES
YARD
M W
SPRING GDNS RD
LAURA
Fountain
JOHNSTONE
OLD KING ST
MILSOM ST
JOHN ST
QUIET ST
OLD BOND ST
NEW BOND ST
GREEN ST
NORTHGATE ST
BRIDGE ST
Library
The
Podium
PLACE
QUEEN
SQUARE
WOOD ST
QUEEN ST
PO
Victoria
Art Gallery
Pulteney
Bridge
Beazer
Maze
Recreation
Ground
PULTENEY ROAD
4
BEAUFORT
SQ
TRIM ST
UPPER BOROUGH WALLS
UNION ST
NORTHUM-
BERLAND PL
HIGH ST
Grand
Parade
ARGYLE ST
Market
Pulteney
Weir
River Trips
Theatre
Royal
M W
BRIDEWELL LA
PARSONAGE LA
THE
CORRIDOR
Guildhall
ORANGE
GROVE
Alkmaar
Gdn
River Avon
Sports &
Leisure Centre
WESTGATE ST
CHEAP ST
ABBEY
CHURCH YD
Abbey
Parade
Gardens
NORTH PARADE ROAD
KINGSMEAD ST
WESTGATE BLDGS
ST
MICHAEL'S
PL
Pump
Room
Roman
Baths &
Museum
YORK ST
River
Trips
DUKE ST
P M W
5
Thermae
Bath
Spa
Hot Bath
STALL STREET
SWALLOW ST
N PDE PASS
Sally
Lunn's
House
PIERRE-
PONT ST
SOUTH PARADE
North Parade
Cricket Ground
KINGSMEAD
SQUARE
HETLING
BATH ST
BILBURY LA
BEAU
GREEN ST
N PDE
PASS
OLD ORCHARD ST
PIERREPONT
PL
PRIVATE
SPRING
SPRING CRES
GDNS
FERRY
LANE
Abbey
Church
House
LOWER BOROUGH WALLS
ABBEYGATE
ST
HENRY ST
Police
Station
AVON ST
ST JAMES'S PARADE
AMERY J
SOUTHGATE
NEW ORCHARD ST
M W
KINGSTON
RD
MANVERS ST
M W
CORN STREET
P
NARROW QUAY
AMBURY
STREET
SOMERSET
ST
MARCHANTS
PASS
NEWARK ST
RAILWAY ST
M W
Bus
Station
RAILWAY PLACE
6
WALKWAY
BROAD QUAY
DORCHESTER ST
Bath Spa Railway
Station
W M
W M
ROSSITER ROAD
Churchill
Bridge
Southgate
Bridge
P
Skew
Bridge
Widcombe
Bridge
Lower
Lock
WELLS RD
LWR BRISTOL RD
WELLS RD
CLAVERTON ST
RD

C   **D**   **E**   **F**

N

JARROLD
publishing

BATH ...MORE THAN A GUIDE

ANNIE BULLEN

CITY-BREAK GUIDES

Front cover:
Pump Room

Previous page:
Roman Baths

The publishers wish to
thank Pat Dunlop and Ann
Steedman (Bath & NE
Somerset Council) and
Linda Simmonds (TIC) for
their invaluable
assistance; also the many
owners of Bath businesses
for their kindness
in allowing us to photo-
graph their premises.

All information correct at
time of going to press but
may be subject to change.

Printed in Singapore.
ISBN 0 7117 2645 0   1/04

Designer:
Simon Borrough
Editor:
Angela Royston
Artwork and walk maps:
Clive Goodyer
City maps:
The Map Studio, Romsey,
Hants. Main map based
on cartography
© George Philip Ltd

Acknowledgements
Photography © Jarrold
Publishing by Neil
Jinkerson.
Additional photography
by kind permission of:
American Museum in
Britain; Bath & NE
Somerset Council; Bath
Industrial Heritage Centre;
Bridgeman Art Library
(Holburne Museum); John
Curtis; Moody Goose
Restaurant; Museum of
East Asian Art; Philip
Pearce; Mark Slade;
Edmund Sumner/VIEW;
Victoria Art Gallery.

CONTENTS

WELCOME TO BATH

They came, they saw — and they were conquered. The Romans, captivated 2,000 years ago by this green valley with its miraculous stream of endless hot water, stayed here for 400 years. The remains of their tremendous bath and temple complex are still a world-class attraction, bringing thousands of visitors to this most elegant of cities. There was a settlement here before the Romans, who tactfully managed to combine the worship of the Celtic god Sulis, with that of their own Minerva. Representations of both gods were found in the ancient temple. The Saxons arrived after the departure of the Romans and gave Bath its present name. Edgar, the first king of all England, was crowned here in a church that stood on the site of the present Abbey.

Royal Crescent

Royal Crescent

Later, the Georgians swept away the medieval muddle and made a beautiful city, built out of local stone and designed on the classical principles of the Palladian style of architecture. Bath became fashionable once more, and the world flocked to take the waters and to enjoy the public entertainment. Business grew around this early tourist trade, enriching the city and adding to its attraction and elegance.

Time doesn't stand still in Bath. Visitors come to admire the legacy of the past, but they also enjoy the vibrancy of the present – the stylish restaurants and shops, the diversity of entertainment, and the unique feel of a city with an exciting past and future.

THAT'S FUNNY

When you walk past Royal Crescent look closely at the great sweep of lawn separating the residents' private area from the beginning of the public park. You can't see a fence, but privacy is protected by a ha-ha – a sunken 'ditch' and wall – originally built, it is said, to prevent grazing cattle from straying into the Crescent.

HIGHLIGHTS

Everyone has heard of the Roman Baths and, of course, they are at the heart of what the city is all about. But, after you've visited this 2,000-year-old complex, there is plenty more to see and do in Bath. Here are some of the top attractions.

Roman Baths

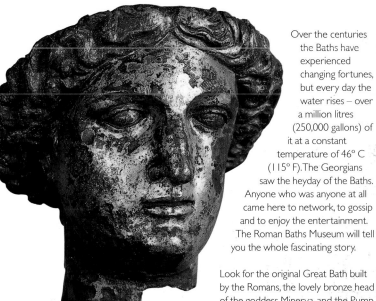

The goddess
Minerva

Over the centuries the Baths have experienced changing fortunes, but every day the water rises – over a million litres (250,000 gallons) of it at a constant temperature of 46° C (115° F). The Georgians saw the heyday of the Baths. Anyone who was anyone at all came here to network, to gossip and to enjoy the entertainment. The Roman Baths Museum will tell you the whole fascinating story.

Look for the original Great Bath built by the Romans, the lovely bronze head of the goddess Minerva, and the Pump Room, completed in 1795.

Open: daily; Jul–Aug: 9.00–21.00 (last exit 22.00); Mar–Jun and Sep–Oct: 9.00–17.00 (last exit 18.00); Nov–Feb: 9.30–16.30 (last exit 17.30). Closed 25 and 26 Dec

Entry: under £10

Further information: pages 46–49

ROMAN BATHS
Abbey Church Yard; map D4

Ever since the leprous Prince Bladud found a miraculous cure for his disfiguring disease by bathing in the hot springs in 863 BC, people have made their way to Bath to take the waters. The Bladud story is a legend, but there's no doubt that the Romans made Bath their base, staying here for nearly 400 years. They built a luxurious spa with baths of varying temperatures, a sauna, exercise rooms, a Turkish bath and cool plunge pools. Spiritual needs were catered for by the construction of a temple, devoted to the worship of their own goddess Minerva, and the Celtic idol, Sulis.

> **TREAT YOURSELF**
> Visit the Pump Room for coffee and a Bath bun in elegant surroundings to the strains of music from the famous Pump Room Trio. If you are able to go at lunchtime you will eat to tunes from the resident pianist.

BATH ABBEY AND THE ABBEY HERITAGE VAULTS

Abbey Church Yard; map D4

You can't miss the Abbey – the church itself, built of Bath's honey-coloured stone, dominates the centre of the city. The paved Abbey Church Yard is where people meet, find refreshments, are entertained by street artists and shop for souvenirs. The Abbey is imposing and full of interest – but its status is that of a parish church.

Look for the charming stone angels clambering up and down the Abbey's west front, the Edgar window inside, above the north choir stall, and the magnificent carved ceilings high above the choir and the nave.

Open: every Sun for six services; visitors: Easter Monday to last Sat in Oct: Mon–Sat 9.00–18.00, Sun 13.15–14.45 and 16.45–17.30; last Sun in Oct to Easter Sunday: Mon–Sat 9.00–16.30, Sun 13.15–14.45

Entry: free, but a donation of £2.50 is suggested

Further information: pages 34–35

Bath Abbey and Olive tree detail

THERMAE BATH SPA
Hot Bath Street; map C5

This magnificent new Spa – with two thermal pools, steam rooms and facilities for massage and other treatments – opened in 2003. Using all three of Bath's natural hot springs, Thermae gives people the chance to 'take the waters' once more, restoring the city's status as one of Europe's leading spas.

Look for the view over Bath and the green hills beyond as you swim in the naturally warm waters of the open-air rooftop pool.

Open: daily; 9.00–22.00 (last admission 20.00)

Entry: from £17 depending on time spent in the Spa

Further information: pages 52–53

The Building of Bath Museum

THE BUILDING OF BATH MUSEUM
The Vineyards, The Paragon; map D1

This exhibition, housed in a charming Gothic chapel, tells how Bath was transformed into the mellow city we enjoy today. One hundred years of architectural innovation, craftsmanship and decoration are celebrated here. Look for the new 18th-century Interiors Gallery, showing the techniques the Georgians employed to achieve all that splendour.

Open: Tue–Sun 10.30–17.00 (last admission 16.15); also open for same hours on bank holiday Mon and Mon during Jul and Aug

Entry: under £5

Further information: page 39

Thermae Bath Spa

TREAT YOURSELF
Bathe in Bath's naturally hot spring water in the rooftop pool at the Thermae Spa and book one of their therapeutic herbal wrap treatments, too.

THE CIRCUS, ROYAL CRESCENT AND NO. 1 ROYAL CRESCENT
map B2 and A1

The perfect circle of the 33 houses in architect John Wood's Palladian-style Circus is bettered only by the magnificent curve of Royal Crescent, designed by his son, also called John. Judge for yourself – the two architectural glories are separated by a short walk along Brock Street. Look for the wonderfully detailed decoration on the Circus houses, and the perfect proportion of the Ionic columns of Royal Crescent. Then visit No. 1 Royal Crescent, restored and redecorated, using authentic materials to recreate that Georgian opulence.

No. 1 Royal Crescent
Open: mid Feb–end Oct: Tue–Sun 10.30–17.00; Nov: Tue–Sun 10.30–16.00 plus two weekends during December. Last admission half an hour before closing
Entry: under £5
Further information: page 50

THE JANE AUSTEN CENTRE
40 Gay Street; map C3

Bath's most famous visitor and sometime-resident Jane Austen professed herself weary of the affectation of Bath society. But she painted a wonderful portrait of it and here you can discover the Bath she knew. Join the walking tours which will show you the places she visited. You can also buy out-of-print editions of her work, and gifts associated with Jane, her books and Georgian Bath.

The Circus and Royal Crescent

Open: daily; Mon–Sat 10.00–17.30; Sun 10.30–17.30
Entry: under £5
Further information: page 41

MUSEUM OF COSTUME AND ASSEMBLY ROOMS
Bennett Street; map C2

The Assembly Rooms in the upper part of Bath were a central point of the Georgian social whirl. And now they share a space with the internationally renowned Museum of Costume, which includes more than 30,000 items of clothing and fashion accessories from the late 16th century to the present day.
Open: daily; Jan–Feb, Nov–Dec 11.00–17.00 (last admission 16.00); Mar–Oct 11.00–18.00 (last admission 17.00). Limited access when in use for functions
Tel: 01225 477785
Entry: around £5
Further information: page 42

PULTENEY BRIDGE
map D3

There are only three shop-lined bridges in the world and this is one of them. As you walk across from Bridge Street to Argyle Street, you'll enjoy not only Bath's unique shops, but also the elegant Palladian design of Robert Adams, conceived more than 220 years ago. Look for the steps on the southern side (in Argyle Street), leading down to the River Avon and the dramatic swirl of the weir.
Further information: page 45

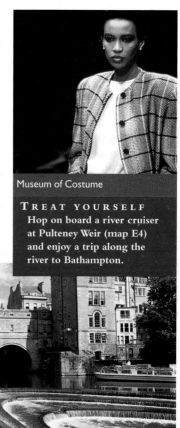

Museum of Costume

TREAT YOURSELF
Hop on board a river cruiser at Pulteney Weir (map E4) and enjoy a trip along the river to Bathampton.

Pulteney Bridge

Prior Park

PRIOR PARK LANDSCAPE GARDEN
Ralph Allen Drive, Combe Down

This garden, owned now by The National Trust but laid out for entrepreneur Ralph Allen (see page 16), has wonderful views across the city of Bath. Look for the romantic Palladian bridge and the grotto, said to have been designed by poet Alexander Pope.

Open: Feb–Oct: Wed–Mon 11.00–17.30 or dusk if earlier; Dec–Jan: Fri–Sun only 11.00–dusk
Entry: under £5
Further information: page 44

A WALK DOWN WALCOT STREET
Map D1–D3

Bath is full of exciting shops (see pages 58–69) but, if you enjoy looking for something a little bit different, spend an hour or so browsing in the shops along this street, which is still referred to as the 'artisans' quarter' of the city.

LUNCH AT THE MOODY GOOSE
7a Kingsmead Square; map C4

This small, independently owned restaurant, which holds a Michelin star and two AA rosettes, uses fresh local produce for its modern English menu. The two- or three-course lunchtime menu includes chargrilled foods, salads and fresh fish. Typical starters include cream of basil and courgette soup with a ravioli of olive and garlic, while you might choose roasted fillet of skate and bacon with shallots braised in red wine and pea purée for your main course.

Open: Mon–Sat for lunch 12.00–13.30; dinner 18.00 onwards

BATH FROM AN OPEN-TOP BUS

Several operators give informative and often funny tours of the city, using double-decker buses. You can hop on and off the bus at different points when you want to visit an attraction.

Tel: 09068 360394 for recorded information on the different tours available

Walcot Reclamation

The Moody Goose

BEAU NASH
AND THE BUILDING
OF BATH

The beautiful Bath we know today,
a city built mainly in one style and
of one material, owes its remarkable
unity of design largely to four men: a
professional gambler and dandy, a
hard-working entrepreneur and two
far-sighted architects.

Richard 'Beau' Nash

THE DANDY

Richard 'Beau' Nash, a drop-out from
the army and the law and a professional
gambler, walked into the tumbledown
country town that was Bath in 1703 –
the same year that Queen Anne
endorsed the health-giving properties of
the water. Nash, becoming Bath's Master
of Ceremonies in 1704, set about changing the city's social structure. Although
he lived for pleasure, he was a stickler
for order. He was responsible for
banishing swords and duelling, devising
sophisticated entertainments, improving
the streets and buildings and developing
Bath's reputation as a safe, civilized and
fashionable place. There's a statue of
Beau Nash in a high alcove in the Pump
Room (see page 46). It's hard to equate
this bewigged, portly and respectable
figure with the gambling, womanizing,
social creature who turned a decaying
town into a place of fashion and fun.

Queen Square

THE ENTREPRENEUR

Ralph Allen, a poor boy made good,
went to work in Bath's post office in
1710. He soon made a tidy sum by
restructuring postal routes across the
whole country. This money was sunk into
an ambitious venture – the rebuilding
of Bath. In 1727 Allen bought the stone
works at Combe Down and commissioned builder and architect John Wood
to design areas of great beauty – all built
with the mellow honey-coloured limestone dug from his quarries.

The Circus frieze

THE ARCHITECTS

In 1727 John Wood the Elder came to Bath and his son, also John Wood, was born here. The father, aflame with enthusiasm for the work of Italian architect Andrea Palladio, wanted to rebuild Bath in Palladian glory. He started straight away, building the beautifully proportioned Queen Square and the North and South Parades, before designing a grand mansion, Prior Park, for Allen.

The Circus (see page 39) came next. Wood's inspiration for this perfectly circular design was Rome's Colosseum. Building began in 1754 – the year that John Wood died, before his dream took shape. But work went on. John Wood the Younger, now an accomplished architect himself, took on his father's ambitious designs – and, some say, surpassed them with his own glorious Royal Crescent (see page 50), completed in 1774.

Prior Park

RULES FOR TAXIS

Beau Nash's passion for order led him to regulate the behaviour and the fares of the unruly sedan-chair owners, the Georgian equivalent of 'taxi drivers'. The regulations that govern taxis today are based on the rules that Nash drew up nearly 300 years ago.

JANE AUSTEN'S BATH

Of all the writers, artists and celebrities who have lived in Bath, none is better known than Jane Austen. Her Bath, and the one we explore 200 years later, are not very different. The heroines of her two 'Bath' novels, the unsophisticated Catherine Morland (*Northanger Abbey*) and the self-effacing Anne Elliot (*Persuasion*), walked the same streets and visited the public buildings that we enjoy today.

Gravel Walk

PEN PORTRAIT
Here is a contemporary description of Jane by her nephew, J.E. Austen-Leigh, one-time vicar of Bray in Berkshire: 'Her figure was rather tall and slender …. In complexion she was a clear brunette with a rich colour; she had full round cheeks, with mouth and nose small and well formed, bright hazel eyes, and brown hair forming natural curls close round her face.'

We can follow the walk taken by Anne and the gallant Captain Wentworth, as he at last declares his frustrated love for her in the final chapters of *Persuasion*. They set out from Union Street to make their way to Camden Place in the upper part of town, by way of the quiet Gravel Walk that skirts The Circus and Royal Crescent. They would have encountered carriages and sedan chairs rather than cars and bicycles, but the streets and the buildings have changed little.

Jane's characters met in the Pump Room for their morning gossip; they danced and went to concerts at the Assembly

Rooms. In Jane's time there were two sets of Rooms – the Upper and the Lower. Four balls a week were held here at the end of the 18th century. Introductions were made by the Master of Ceremonies, which is how young Catherine Morland met Henry Tilney, her hero, at a ball in the Lower Rooms.

Two long visits to Bath at the end of the 18th century, and five years' residence from 1801 to 1806, gave Jane Austen more than a nodding acquaintance with the city whose characters, social life, streets and buildings she observed so well. Although she took part in all that Bath afforded by way of entertainment and amusement, she was by nature a watcher and an observer. Those observations of smart Georgian society were not always kind, as Jane took sideways swipes at the snobbery and pretension she saw on all sides.

She lived at various addresses in Bath, including Sydney Street and Gay Street, near the present-day Jane Austen Centre (see page 41), which tells the full story of her life in the city. Gay Street, situated between Queen Square and The Circus, was evidently a good address – in *Persuasion* that arch-snob Sir Walter Elliot is relieved to find his tenants, Admiral and Mrs Croft, are staying there, so that he need not be ashamed to visit them: 'The Crofts had placed themselves in lodgings in Gay-street, perfectly to Sir Walter's satisfaction.'

RECREATING THE PAST

Is this the real Jane Austen? This portrait was painted by forensic artist Melissa Dring, who researched contemporary accounts of the writer's appearance before she began work. It was unveiled at the Jane Austen Centre in Bath in December 2002.

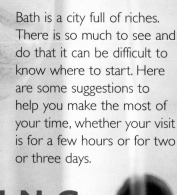

Bath is a city full of riches. There is so much to see and do that it can be difficult to know where to start. Here are some suggestions to help you make the most of your time, whether your visit is for a few hours or for two or three days.

PLANNING YOUR VISIT

MIRACLE CURE

In the past, people came to Bath for all sorts of reasons – many of them medical. This is not surprising when you read the list of ailments the water was said to cure: gout, rheumatism, palsies, asthma, convulsions, the itch, jaundice, scab, leprosy, scrofula, epilepsy, eye problems, deafness, palpitations, ulcers, piles, infertility – and many more.

WHAT TO DO ON THE FIRST DAY

Bath exists because of its unique thermal springs, harnessed for human use by the Romans nearly 2,000 years ago. If you have only one day in the city, go to see the remains of that impressive Roman bathing complex, linked to a massive temple where the goddess Minerva was worshipped. Before or after your visit to the Roman Baths (see page 46) be sure to take coffee and a Bath bun, and even a glass of the famous water, in the adjoining Pump Room (see page 46).

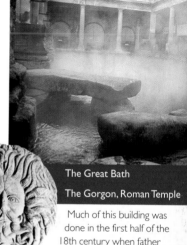

The Great Bath

The Gorgon, Roman Temple

Take time for a look at the street entertainers and a browse around the shops in Abbey Church Yard before an exploration of the Abbey itself (see page 34), built of the same honey-coloured limestone as the rest of the city.

Before lunch stroll across to Pulteney Bridge (see page 45), one of only three in the world built as a complete shopping street. Then have a leisurely lunch at one of Bath's many good pubs and restaurants (see pages 70–79) and enjoy a wander through the interesting small streets and passages in the city centre.

You'll notice that most of the houses and shops are built of mellow Bath stone.

Much of this building was done in the first half of the 18th century when father and son architects, both named John Wood, were fulfilling their dream of rebuilding Bath in the classical Palladian style (see pages 16–17). If you walk to the upper town you can enjoy the older man's masterpiece, the perfectly symmetrical Circus, and his son's grand design, the nearby Royal Crescent (see page 50).

Many famous people have lived and worked in Bath, but none is more synonymous with the city than Jane Austen (see pages 18–19), whose novels *Persuasion* and *Northanger Abbey* tell us as much about the geography of Bath as they do of its social fabric. The Jane Austen Centre (see page 41) will give you a vivid picture of Jane's Bath and of the novelist herself.

WHAT TO DO IN THE NEXT TWO OR THREE DAYS

You've seen the heart of Bath, including some of the great buildings and historical sites that tell you why and how the city has developed into the lovely and lively place it is today. If you have longer than one day to spend here, what you do now depends on your own tastes – and there's no doubt you'll find something to satisfy them. Here are some 'pick and mix' suggestions to help you enjoy your stay.

Take the waters

Bathing in the only natural hot spring water in Britain is possible once more with the opening of the Thermae Bath Spa (see page 52), built on the site of some of the old baths. You can book in for a couple of hours for a swim in the open-air rooftop pool, or take longer and enjoy some of the relaxing treatments in this up-to-the-minute spa.

Shopping spree

Bath is a shopper's paradise with hundreds of independently owned stores selling unusual goods. Follow our shoppers' walk (see page 28), or do a little exploration yourself using the shopping guide on pages 58–69. Walcot Street is a good place to start for real variety – from delicious cheese and gourmet goodies to wild and wacky pottery, knitwear, furniture, antiques, hats and toys. They do good coffee there too.

Doolally's (page 71)

Walcot Woollies (page 59)

Explore the art

Both the Holburne Museum of Art (page 41) and the Victoria Art Gallery (page 54) have extensive collections, much of the work relating to Bath. Gainsborough lived in Bath, painting the society portraits displayed here. To reach the Holburne Museum from the Victoria you must cross Pulteney Bridge – a work of art itself. Although the collections in the Museum of East Asian Art (see page 42) have little to do with the city, they are the most important of their kind in the country – and probably the world.

Enjoy the past

The past is all around you in Bath, but you can get an insight into the integrity of the craftsmanship that went into the building and decoration of the city by visiting museums run by the Bath Preservation Trust. The Building of Bath Museum (see page 39) housed in a lovely Gothic chapel, shows how the buildings were built, decorated and used, while No. 1 Royal Crescent (see page 50) has been restored in authentic period detail. Different tastes are displayed at Beckford's Tower (see page 38), with a museum housing the collection of 18th-century eccentric, William Beckford. A more humble view of domestic life in Bath is shown at the former home of musicians and astronomers, William and Caroline Herschel (see page 54).

HEIGHT OF FASHION

The craze for eye-catching hairstyles peaked in the 1770s when fops flaunted bizarre creations up to 150cm (5 feet) tall. They used wire frames covered with horsehair glued in place with lard and egg white. But, if they stood too near candlelit chandeliers in the Assembly Rooms, things could get rather hot – and sometimes downright dangerous.

Victoria Art Gallery

Le Beaujolais

Dress sense

You'll need at least two hours to enjoy all that the Museum of Costume (see page 42) has to offer with its unique collection of clothes that have been the talk of the fashion world for over 400 years. While you're in that part of town why not work your way down Bartlett Street for a good browse in the many antique and curiosity shops, finishing with lunch in Woods in Alfred Street or the equally popular Le Beaujolais in Chapel Row (see pages 73 and 74)?

Mix and match
Set out on one of the walks on pages 26–31 designed to give a taste of what Bath has to offer, not only as a city of historical importance but also as a place to enjoy today.

Bath al fresco
Visit the Bath Deli in Margaret's Buildings or The Fine Cheese Co. in Walcot Street and put together a picnic. Enjoy it in one of Bath's many parks or gardens (see pages 56–57) or make your way to Prior

> **TREAT YOURSELF**
> Take youngsters to Café Cadbury in Union Street, where they can indulge their taste for chocolate.

Royal Victoria Park

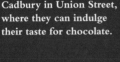

The Fine Cheese Co.

Park (see page 44), the lovely landscape garden just outside the city, where picnickers are welcome. You can hire bicycles or simply rise above it all and book a ride in a hot-air balloon (see page 83) to see Bath from an entirely different perspective. Or hire a punt (basic tuition given) from the Bath Boating Station (see page 82) and float lazily down the river for an hour or so.

Bath Boating Station

American dream
The only thing British about the American Museum (see page 33) at Claverton Manor is the house itself, but its worth a visit for the carefully recreated period furnished rooms, showing the development of American domestic life over the centuries. American visitors might enjoy the home cooking and a nostalgic glimpse of their past, but all will marvel at those pioneers, who set out from England centuries ago.

WALKS

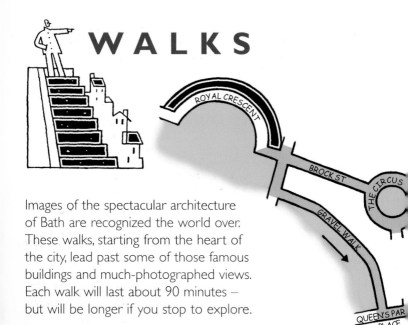

Images of the spectacular architecture of Bath are recognized the world over. These walks, starting from the heart of the city, lead past some of those famous buildings and much-photographed views. Each walk will last about 90 minutes – but will be longer if you stop to explore.

BEAUTIFUL BATH WALK

Start in the Abbey Church Yard with its buskers, shops and cafés. Here you'll find the Roman Baths (see page 46), the Abbey (see page 34) and the Pump Room.

Cross York Street towards Abbey Green and turn down North Parade Passage, passing Sally Lunn's (see page 51). Carry straight on, along North Parade Road, and over the bridge. Once across, go down the left-hand steps to walk alongside the Avon and the weir, up to Pulteney Bridge (see page 45). Climb the steps, turning left over Pulteney Bridge, towards the city centre.

Royal Crescent

Once over Bridge Street follow Northgate Street into Broad Street, past the Postal Museum (see page 38) and Shire's Yard. Turn down George Street on your left and take the next right, Bartlett Street, which is full of antique shops.

Cross Alfred Street to Bennett Street where you'll find the Assembly Rooms and Museum of Costume (see page 42). A left turn takes you past the Museum of East Asian Art (see page 42) and into John Wood's glorious Circus (see page 39). Continue along Brock Street until you reach Royal Crescent (see page 50). Turn left onto the path and left again along Gravel Walk to Queen's Parade Place and Queen Square, another architectural tour de force.

From Queen Square turn into Wood Street and right into Queen Street and then into Bridewell Lane. Cross Westgate Street towards the elegantly colonnaded Bath Street, built to link the three hot baths. It's a short step to the new Thermae Bath Spa (see page 52) and back to the Abbey Church Yard.

Abbey Church Yard

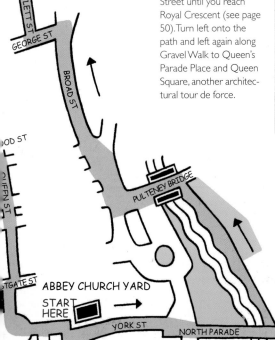

ASSEMBLY ROOMS

ETT ST

BARTLETT ST

GEORGE ST

BROAD ST

OD ST

UEEN ST

PULTENEY BRIDGE

TGATE ST

ABBEY CHURCH YARD

START HERE

YORK ST

NORTH PARADE

Guildhall Market

STOPPING TO SHOP WALK

Bath has some of the best shops (see pages 58–69) in the country. This walk won't take you to all of them, but will give you an idea of what's on offer – and you'll find plenty of stopping-off points for cups of coffee or something a little stronger. The walk will take anything from an hour to a whole day, depending on how much shopping you can manage.

We'll start at the top end of handsome Milsom Street and walk down to Jolly's, opened in 1831 as The Bath Emporium. At the bottom of Milsom Street, turn right into Quiet Street and Wood Street. Continue to charming Queen Street before moving on to Trim Street. Then turn left into Upper Borough Walls and keep going until you see

Union Passage. A network of small shopping lanes opens here – visit Northumberland Place and The Corridor, before emerging at the other end to call into the Guildhall Market, just opposite The Corridor, and then turn left heading towards Northgate Street.

At this point, divert to see Pulteney Bridge (see page 45) – more than a mere river crossing, it is one of the very few bridges in the world lined with shops.

Cross back into Bridge Street and, at the end, turn right and keep going until you reach Walcot Street. It's a good idea to keep to the right-hand side of the street as the walk brings you back down the other side. On the way back, turn left into Broad Street via Saracen Street. When you've explored Broad Street's shops, turn into Shire's Yard, by the Postal Museum, and so back into Milsom Street.

Meet one of the expert
guides outside the Pump
Room at 10.30 for an
informative, free, two-
hour exploration of the
city, before taking time
for a leisurely lunch at
one of Bath's many
excellent restaurants
(see pages 71–77).

Pulteney Bridge

PEOPLE AND PLACES WALK

Bath, probably the most elegant city in Britain, has always lured the rich and famous. No blue plaques here – instead elegantly engraved bronze tablets show where celebrities once lived. The walk starts at Sawclose and takes you to out-of-the-way corners as well as through Bath's best-known streets.

Richard 'Beau' Nash (see page 16) had more than one house in the city, but a bronze plaque on the wall of Popjoys, the house of his mistress, next to the Theatre Royal, commemorates his name. Walk up to Queen Square where the two John Woods, father and son (see page 17), were proud to live in houses they had designed. Wood the Elder's tablet is on No. 24, while his son's house was at No. 41 Gay Street, facing the Square.

Continue around the Square to New King Street. Astronomers and musicians William and Caroline Herschel's home at No. 19 is now a museum (see page 54), while playwright Richard Brinsley Sheridan lived at what is now No. 9 (his old house was pulled down for redevelopment). Sheridan caused enormous scandal when he eloped to France with the beautiful 18-year-old singer Elizabeth Linley, with whom all of Bath was said to be infatuated.

Return to Queen Square and follow Gravel Walk to reach the Linley home in Royal Crescent, where the elopement is commemorated on the wall of No. 11. Their story was not a happy one, however. Sheridan found fame but was reckless with his fortune, while Elizabeth, saddened by his infidelity, died of consumption in 1792, aged 38. Further on, at No. 17, there's a tablet for shorthand supremo, Sir Isaac Pitman.

Walk along Brock Street to The Circus, which is full of tablets. Gainsborough lived and worked at No. 17, while Lord Clive of India's plaque hangs on No. 14. One-time Prime Minister, William Pitt the Elder, later the Earl of Chatham, resided further along, at No. 7.

Leave by Gay Street. Jane Austen lived at No. 25, now a dentist's surgery, for a while, although her tablet is on No. 4 Sydney Place (map F2). Continue along George Street to The Paragon and No. 33, where actress Sarah Siddons lived for several years. If you have the energy, take the steep steps opposite Hay Hill down to Walcot Street to visit Walcot Church where Jane Austen's father, the Revd George Austen, is buried. Novelist Fanny Burney, who lived at South Parade, is also buried here.

Paragon Steps

ACCORDING TO TASTE

Charles Dickens, whose novels chronicled life in the 19th century, satirized Bath in *The Pickwick Papers*, where Mr Pickwick stays in Royal Crescent and takes the waters. His servant, Sam Weller, was not so certain about Bath's famous liquid cure, saying that it had 'a wery strong flavour o' warm flat irons'.

Turn back towards Saracen Street. The pub on the corner, The Saracen's Head, is where the young Charles Dickens stayed during his days in Bath as a newspaper reporter.

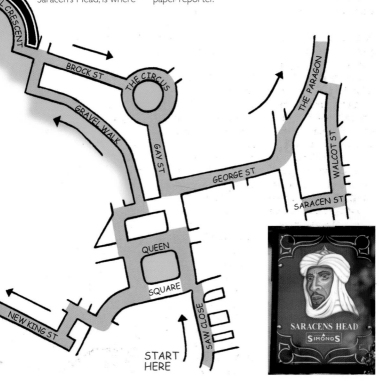

SARACENS HEAD
SIMONDS

START HERE

The joy of Bath is the diversity of things to see and do. Of course there's much to find out about the Roman Baths and the city's favourite writer, Jane Austen, but other interests, from astronomy to fine art and fashion, are all catered for. What's more, nothing is very far away in this small city, which is so easy to explore on foot.

American Museum at Claverton Manor

SIGHTSEEING

American Museum
Claverton Manor, Claverton Down

This early 19th-century manor house contains the finest collection of American art outside the United States. A series of rooms is furnished with original material from 17th-century colonial days to the end of the 19th century. Different cultural traditions, from English Puritan to Spanish colonists, are represented and you can enjoy dramatic re-enactments of important events in American history (telephone for details). 'Christmas at Claverton' each year demonstrates period decoration. Other galleries show the work of American craftsmen and women. The gardens are also open to visitors.

DON'T MISS
Display of American quilts from those made

by early settlers to more complicated, later designs.

The Shaker Room with examples of classic design and furniture.

The Mount Vernon Garden – a replica of George Washington's own garden.

Getting there: signed from city centre up Bathwick Hill and from A36. Or take No. 18 bus from Bath; get off at The Avenue just before the University – museum is 10-minute walk from here

Open: 20 Mar–31 Oct: Tue–Thu gardens 13.00–18.00, museum 14.00–17.00; Fri–Sun gardens 12.00–18.00, museum 14.00–17.00. Open bank holiday Mon and Mons in Aug

Entry: admission to main museum under £10; gardens and outside galleries under £5

Tel: 01225 460503

Website: www.americanmuseum.org

Disabled access: limited

Other facilities: shop and tea room

American Museum

Bath Abbey
Abbey Church Yard; map D4

Bath's parish church is known as the 'Lantern of the West' because of the light flooding its interior through many windows. The 500-year-old church is an abbey in name only, having lost its status in 1539, when Henry VIII ordered the dissolution of the monasteries.

Although this is the third church to have been built on this site, it can still claim the kudos of being the place chosen by Edgar, the first king of all England, for his coronation in 973. The coronation service we know now is based on that one, devised more than 1,000 years ago. Edgar's coronation took place in a small Saxon church. That was replaced by an enormous cathedral, so big that the present abbey could have fitted in its nave. That too fell into disrepair, to be rebuilt by statesman and, later, Bishop of Bath, Oliver King in 1499.

Things came to a disastrous pass for the new abbey in 1539, when Henry VIII gave orders for its destruction, along with many others in the country. His daughter Queen Elizabeth I later turned the tables, urging its restoration, which was completed in 1611, when Bath Abbey started its long service as the city's parish church.

The founder's vision

The charming carved stone angels clambering up and down ladders on the west

Bath Abbey and the Edgar window

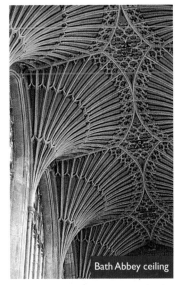

Bath Abbey ceiling

while the Abbey was still suffering from the damage inflicted by Henry VIII, James Montague found himself Bishop of Bath and Wells. Eventually, out of his own fortune, he paid for the nave to be re-roofed. Although he was 'promoted' to become Bishop of Winchester, he retained his affection for Bath and provided for his body to be buried in the church. The wonderful stonework above the nave is a 19th-century copy of the Vertue brothers' glorious craftsmanship.

DON'T MISS

The carved stone angels clambering up and down ladders on the west front, and the olive tree on the outermost buttresses of the front.
The magnificent fan vaulting in the chancel and above the nave.
The Montague tomb in the centre of the Abbey.
The Edgar window on the east wall of the church at the end of the north choir aisle. It shows the crowning ceremony of Edgar, the first king of all England, by Archbishops Dunstan and Oswald on Whit Sunday 973.

front were the vision of the Abbey's founder and first bishop, Oliver King. He is said to have dreamed in 1499 of angels toiling up and down a ladder between heaven and earth. By the ladder was an olive tree. Oliver King, a highly placed official at the court of Henry VII, took his dream, with the olive tree symbolizing his name, as a sign he must rebuild Bath's church. You can see the olive tree encircled by a king's crown and topped with a Bishop's mitre on the outermost buttresses of the front.

Carved ceilings

The earlier Tudor vaulting at the eastern end of the church, in the chancel, was created by brothers and master masons Robert and William Vertue. In 1608,

Open: every Sun for six services; visitors: Easter Monday to last Sat in Oct: Mon–Sat 9.00–18.00, Sun 13.15–14.45 and 16.45–17.30; last Sun in Oct to Easter Sunday: Mon–Sat 9.00–16.30, Sun 13.15–14.45
Entry: free, but a suggested donation of £2.50 will help maintain the church
Tel: 01225 422462/446300
Website: www.bathabbey.org
Disabled access: full
Other facilities: bookshop, open Mon–Sat 10.00–16.00

Bath Abbey Heritage Vaults
Abbey Church Yard; map D4

The museum, in cellars alongside Bath Abbey, tells the story of the religious establishments on this site since the 7th century AD. The exhibition begins dramatically with a copy of a 4th-century petition and curse rescued from the Roman Baths in which one Annianus, suspecting that a Christian may have stolen his purse, scratched a curse on a piece of lead, rolled it up and threw it into the hot spring, asking the goddess Sulis Minerva for help. This is England's first written reference to the word 'Christian'.

Open: Mon–Sat 10.00–16.00 (last admission 15.30). Closed Sun, Good Friday and during Christmas week
Entry: under £5

Tel: 01225 422462/446300
Website: www.bathabbey.org
Disabled access: full

Bath Aqua Theatre of Glass
105–107 Walcot Street; map D1

Here you can watch glass of all types being blown and learn about this ancient craft. Stained glass is always being made and the history of glass making is described in the museum. The gift shop sells glass, handmade on the premises.

Open: daily; 10.00–17.00; evenings by arrangement
Entry: under £5
Tel: 01225 428146
Website: www.bathglasstheatre.com
Disabled access: full
Other facilities: shop and children's activities

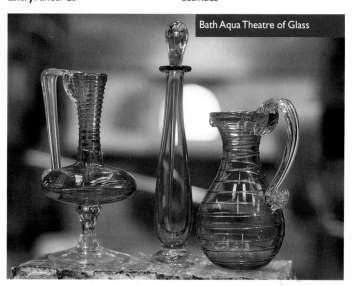
Bath Aqua Theatre of Glass

SHOCKING GOINGS-ON

Writer Daniel Defoe was shocked by what he saw in the Abbey Church Yard more than 300 years ago. He described it as a place of 'raffling, gaming and levity'. These days there's a lot going on outside the Abbey, but you're more likely to be entertained than shocked by the musicians, jugglers and mime artists who gather there.

Bath Industrial Heritage Centre

Julian Road; map C1

The Heritage Centre gives a good picture of working life in Victorian Bath, far removed from the upper-class elegance of the Pump Room and Royal Crescent. Mr Jonathan Burdett Bowler opened his business in 1872 as engineer, brass founder, bell-hanger, gas fitter and locksmith. He also ran a fizzy-drinks factory (making Bath Punch, Cherry Ciderette, Orange Champagne and Hot Tom), and he made and repaired soda water machinery. His business closed in 1969 – and in all those years nothing was thrown out. Here you'll see a faithful recreation of the factory where Mr Bowler and his family tackled any job, from mending a pony harness to casting a part for the new-fangled motor car.

Open: daily; Easter–31 Oct: 10.00–16.30; 1 Nov–Easter: Sat and Sun only 10.00–16.30; other times by appointment
Entry: under £5
Tel: 01225 318348
Website: www.bath-at-work.org.uk
Disabled access: limited
Other facilities: café, shop, children's events and activities

Bath Industrial Heritage Centre

Victorian letter box

Bath Postal Museum
8 Broad Street; map D3
One hundred years ago you could send an invitation to tea or dinner on the day of writing – and expect a reply. Up to seven postal deliveries were made each day and letters were the preferred method of communication for many. This museum, built on the spot where the world's first letter to bear a postage stamp, the Penny Black, was sent in 1840, tells the story of letter writing, the carriage and delivery of mail, and everything to do with postal systems. There is also a children's activity room.
Open: Mar–Oct: Mon–Sat 11.00–17.00; Nov–Feb: Mon–Sat 11.00–16.30; Sun by request for large parties
Entry: under £5
Tel: 01225 460333
Website: www.bathpostalmuseum.org
Disabled access: limited

Beckford's Tower and Museum
Lansdown Road
Make the effort to see this gloriously individual building, just outside the city. William Beckford (1760–1844) was a wealthy and eccentric scholar and writer who spent his considerable talent and financial resources on collecting and travelling – and building towers. Lansdown Tower – or Beckford's Tower as it is known – was built in 1827 as a study-retreat for his later years. He already owned a house in Lansdown Crescent when he laid out a series of gardens and landscaped features along a mile-long (1.6-kilometre) ride to the summit of Lansdown Hill. At the end of this ride he built a 120-foot (37-metre) high tower with a magnificent belvedere crowned by an octagonal lantern. Inside was a series of sumptuous rooms filled with many pieces of furniture and works of art designed and commissioned by Beckford himself. The Tower has been restored and is open to visitors.
Getting there: park at the Lansdown Park and Ride – the Tower is visible and a 7-minute walk away. From the city centre take the No. 2 bus (702 on Sundays) towards Ensleigh and get off by the MoD facility. Or walk the 3 km (1.5 miles) to the Tower from the city centre, along Lansdown Road
Open: Easter–end Oct: Sat, Sun and bank holiday Mon 10.30–17.00 (last admission 16.30)
Entry: under £5
Information line: 01225 422212
Tel: 01225 460705
Website:
www.bath-preservation-trust.org.uk

The Building of Bath Museum

The Vineyards, The Paragon; map D1

How did the transformation of Bath from small provincial spa into its full Georgian splendour come about? This exhibition, housed in a striking Gothic chapel, tells you. One hundred years of architectural innovation, craftsmanship and decoration are celebrated in the museum's galleries.

The new 18th-century Interiors Gallery is concerned with Georgian taste and room arrangement. It shows how the different techniques, from gilding and lacquering, and furniture making to wallpaper manufacture, were achieved.

DON'T MISS

The 18th-century Interiors Gallery. Visitors are encouraged to handle materials in this exhibition.

Open: Tue–Sun 10.30–17.00 (last admission 16.15); also open for same hours on bank holiday Mon and Mon during Jul and Aug
Entry: under £5
Tel: 01225 333895
Website:
www.bath-preservation-trust.org.uk

Disabled access: limited
Other facilities: gift shop

The Circus

map B2

Architect John Wood (see page 17) had a grand vision of sweeping away Bath's medieval squalor and replacing it with a great Roman-style city. He conceived The Circus, 33 inward-facing houses built in grand Palladian style, arranged in a perfect circle.

DON'T MISS

The detailed decoration, from the perfectly matched three tiers of paired columns (Doric at street level, Ionic in the middle and Corinthian at the top) to the carved stone acorns which adorn the parapets.
A carved stone frieze at first-floor level represents the achievements of the time.

The Circus

The Guildhall
High Street; map D4

The magnificent banqueting room at the Guildhall can be seen when it is not being used for functions. The beautifully proportioned room has portraits by William Hoare and from the studio of Joshua Reynolds, and is lit by three Whitefriars glass chandeliers.

Open: Mon–Thu 9.00–17.00, Fri 9.00–16.30. Closed Sat and Sun and when in use for functions

Entry: free, but there is a box for voluntary donations

Tel: 01225 477724

Disabled access: full

The Guildhall
Hitchcocks' Gallery

Hitchcocks' Gallery
10 Chapel Row, Queen Square; map B4

There are many who will not be able to resist the extraordinary toys, mainly for grown-ups, in the shop and gallery. Cleverly designed and worked by handles and weights, contemporary automata, folk and mechanical toys from Britain, Germany and the Czech republic are often snapped up as soon as they're displayed. You can also buy wooden toys for real children.

Ring to check opening times – they are always open during exhibitions and they will open up by appointment.

Open: Tue–Sat 11.00–17.00 during exhibitions, Fri–Sat always open 11.00–17.00; other times by appointment

Entry: free

Tel: 01225 330646

Website: www.hitchcocks-bath.co.uk

Disabled access: none

Holburne Museum of Art

Open: mid Feb–mid Dec: Tue–Sat
10.00–17.00, Sun 12.30–17.30. Closed
Mon except for group bookings by
appointment. Closed mid Dec–mid Feb
Entry: under £5
Tel: 01225 466669
Website: www.bath.ac.uk/Holburne
Disabled access: full
Other facilities: licensed teahouse,
book and gift shop, free car park and
guided tours by arrangement

Holburne Museum of Art
Great Pulteney Street; map F2

It is interesting to speculate that that
great observer, Jane Austen, might have
cast a vigilant eye over the comings and
goings at this building when it was the
fashionable Sydney Hotel. She and her
family took lodgings at Sydney Place
opposite. Now the comings and goings
are those of art-lovers eager to enjoy
the fine collections of paintings, silver,
bronzes, porcelain, glass, portrait miniatures, maiolica ware and furniture. The
museum was established in 1916 to
house the art belonging to collector
Sir William Holburne.

DON'T MISS

Angelica Kauffmann's haunting portrait
of Henrietta Laura Pulteney (above)
after whom nearby streets are named.
Hone's miniature of Beau Nash, Bath's
much-lauded Master of Ceremonies
(see page 16).
Lunch or coffee at the museum's
celebrated teahouse.

The Jane Austen Centre
40 Gay Street; map C3

'Who can ever be tired of Bath?' asks
Catherine Morland, the unsophisticated
heroine of Jane Austen's *Northanger
Abbey*, a clever book that sets out to
mock gently the popular Gothic novels
of the time. There is an answer to that
question: Jane herself grew tired of the
noise and bustle of the city and of the
pretentiousness of many of its inhabi-
tants. For all that, she paints a compre-
hensive picture of the dinners, the balls,
the assemblies, the matchmaking and the
promenading that made Bath the centre
of the universe for the rich and fashionable of her time. The Jane Austen Centre
tells you much about Jane herself, the
Bath that came within her scrutiny, and of
the importance of the city in her life and
her novels.

Open: daily; Mon–Sat 10.00–17.30, Sun
10.30–17.30
Entry: under £5
Tel: 01225 443000
Website: www.janeausten.co.uk
Disabled access: wheelchair access
to most parts
Other facilities: gift shop

Museum of Costume and Assembly Rooms
Bennett Street; map C2

When Bath was the top people's playground in the 18th century, the place to see and be seen was the Assembly Rooms. Here was where the Georgian carriage-set disported themselves, dancing, taking tea, flirting and playing cards in a purpose-built entertainment centre. It's fitting that the lower ground floor of the Assembly Rooms houses the internationally renowned Museum of Costume, showing not only the magnificent gowns of Georgian England but also highlights of a collection of more than 30,000 items of clothing and fashion accessories from the late 16th century to the present day. Free audioguides explain the changing styles and fashions that you see in the exhibits.

Museum of Costume

Open: daily; Jan–Feb, Nov–Dec 11.00–17.00 (last admission 16.00); Mar–Oct 11.00–18.00 (last admission 17.00). Limited access when in use for functions
Entry: around £5
Tel: 01225 477785/477789
Website: www.museumofcostume.co.uk
Disabled access: full
Other facilities: gift shop and a fashion bookshop

Museum of East Asian Art
12 Bennett Street; map C2

One of the finest collections of Chinese, Korean, Mongolian, Tibetan, Thai and Japanese treasures in the world is housed here in a restored Georgian building. The pieces on show date from around 5000 BC to the 21st century. They are shown in four galleries. A fifth space is used for temporary exhibitions. The emphasis is on education with an active events programme and workshops for adults and children.

Open: daily; Tue–Sat and bank holiday Mon 10.00–17.00; Sun 12.00–17.00
Entry: under £5
Tel: 01225 464640
Website: www.bath.co.uk/musumeastasianart
Disabled access: full
Other facilities: gift shop, introductory video and children's worksheets

Assembly Rooms

Popjoys Restaurant
Beau Nash House, Sawclose; map C4
You'll find Popjoys in guides for the quality of its food, but this restaurant is doubly interesting in that it's set in the house built in 1720 by the celebrated Beau Nash (see page 16) for his long-time mistress Juliana Popjoy. Nash, a notorious gambler, had to move in with Juliana when he gambled his own house away. He died here in 1761.
Open: Restaurant hours for lunch and dinner. Best to book
Tel: 01225 460494
Website: www.popjoys.co.uk

Prior Park Landscape Garden
Ralph Allen Drive, Combe Down
Ralph Allen (see page 16) was the postal official turned entrepreneur who made his fortune supplying the mellow limestone from which most of Bath is built. Prior Park is the grand mansion designed for him by architect John Wood. The house is now an independent school but the gardens, designed with the help of Capability Brown and the poet Alexander Pope, have been restored.

DON'T MISS
The romantic Palladian bridge, one of only four in the world.
The grotto.
The views from many parts of the garden across the city of Bath.
The tranquillity.
Getting there: by public transport or on foot – car parking for disabled only. Frequent bus services from the city centre
Open: Feb–Oct: Wed–Mon 11.00–17.30 or dusk if earlier; Dec–Jan: Fri–Sun only 11.00–dusk
Entry: under £5
Tel: 01225 833422
Website: www.nationaltrust.org.uk
Disabled access: limited wheelchair access to viewpoints
Other facilities: events including guided walks (please telephone); picnickers welcome

Bust of David Garrick in Sawclose

Pulteney Bridge

Pulteney Bridge
map D3

You will no doubt walk across this Palladian bridge, which has been largely restored to Robert Adams' original vision. The bridge over the Avon joined the city to the rural estate of Bathwick, inherited by Frances Pulteney in 1767.

It was built to Adams' elegant design in 1773, but altered over the years. Much of the façade has now been restored and the bridge, one of only three worldwide to be lined with shops, is a major attraction, not only for its history and architecture, but also for the bustle of shoppers and sightseers.

Pump Room
Abbey Church Yard; map D4

In 1706 the whole of fashionable Bath came daily to the Pump Room, to take the waters and listen to gossip. Today's elegant room, overlooking the Great Bath, was opened in 1795. 'Water is Best' reads the Greek inscription, though some may take a sip or two and disagree. Morning coffee, afternoon tea, lunch and Bath buns are all served here to the strains of the Pump Room Trio, or a resident pianist. Two sedan chairs – the taxis of Jane Austen's time – and Thomas Tompion's long-case clock are on display in the Pump Room. The fare for the chairs was a flat 6d (2.5p) – more if hilly – while the clock, dating from 1709, shows the difference between solar time and mean time.

Open: daily; Mar–Jun and Sep–Oct: 9.00–17.00 (last admission); Jul–Aug: 9.00–21.00 (last admission); Jan–Feb and Nov–Dec: 9.30–16.30 (last admission)

Entry: free

Tel: 01225 477785

Website: www.romanbaths.co.uk

Disabled access: full

Pump Room

Roman Baths
Abbey Church Yard; map D4

This is what Bath is all about. Over a million litres (a quarter of a million gallons) of hot water wells up each day from three springs. The Romans couldn't believe their luck 2,000 years ago, so they built a temple and baths where they could practise religious ritual and enjoy the sacred waters. These are the only hot water springs in Britain and the water you see today first fell as rain on the Mendip Hills many thousands of years ago. We all like to throw votive offerings – generally coins – into pools of water and the Celts, who came to Bath before the Romans, were no exception. Archaeologists know that the Celts worshipped their goddess Sulis at this miraculous spring.

Pump Room

Roman Baths

Ritual and relaxation

When the Romans arrived they developed an enormous bathing and temple complex over nearly four centuries, devoting their worship to their own goddess of healing, the wise Minerva, and, tactfully, to the Celtic Sulis, too. The settlement around came to be known as Aquae Sulis – Waters of Sulis – although the impressive temple, supported by four massive columns, was dedicated to both Sulis and Minerva. From the central pediment glared down the gorgon-like head of the Celtic god, while the graceful bronze Minerva held sway inside, bathed in the light of a constantly lit flame. The Romans liked their baths at different temperatures, so that they could work up a sweat before the dirt was scraped from their bodies. They then enjoyed a refreshing plunge into cooler water.

Restoration

But things deteriorated during medieval times. The Romans long gone and the baths silted over, it took a Bishop, John de Villula, to rebuild the bathing pool. He constructed the King's Bath over the Roman reservoir. The Bishop intended the new bath for the use of the sick, as the water was said to have excellent healing properties. But, the Middle Ages being what they were, historians tell us that many squalid scenes of nude bathing and bawdy goings-on, with crowds of jeering spectators, took place there.

The Georgians restored propriety and the baths themselves, so that a visit to Bath to take the waters and be at the centre of society became the fashionable thing to do. Excellent audioguides take you round the whole huge temple and bathing complex. Get your breath back in the exquisitely civilized Georgian Pump Room where you can nibble at a Bath bun, drink coffee and listen to the musical trio. If you're feeling brave, buy a glass of the famous water – you might even like it!

DON'T MISS

The beautiful original bronze head of Minerva, the Roman goddess of wisdom. It was found by workman digging out a sewer in Stall Street in 1727.

The original Roman Great Bath with the well-preserved bases of the pillars that once supported a domed roof.

The elegant Pump Room.

Open: daily; Jul–Aug: 9.00–21.00 (last exit 22.00); Mar–Jun and Sep–Oct: 9.00–17.00 (last exit 18.00); Nov–Feb: 9.30–16.30 (last exit 17.30). Closed 25 and 26 Dec

Entry: under £10

Tel: 01225 477785

Website: www.romanbaths.co.uk

Disabled access: disabled visitors admitted free to terrace overlooking the Great Bath

Other facilities: gift shop and refreshments in Pump Room (see page 46)

King Bladud, who first discovered the waters' healing powers

No. I Royal Crescent
Royal Crescent; map A I

Bath's magnificent Royal Crescent, a tremendous sweep of Palladian-style buildings overlooking the city, is the finest architectural feature of its kind in Europe. As you turn into the Crescent, built between 1767 and 1775, from Brock Street, the sheer grandeur and scale of the buildings will take your breath away. The 30 glorious houses, decorated with a façade of Ionic columns and built of the mellow honey-gold Bath stone, make a semi-elliptical sweep of 150 metres (500 feet). Before them lies a long slope of green lawns. But you can see more than the outside of these wonderful houses, built to the design of architect John Wood the Younger.

No. I Royal Crescent, completed in 1769, was leased to Thomas Brock in that year. Numerous distinguished visitors, including the Duke of York, son of George III, have lived in the house. Later, No. I suffered a decline in fortune, becoming a lodging house by 1968. But it was rescued and given to the Bath Preservation Trust, who restored and redecorated it using only materials available in the 18th century. Now the headquarters of the Trust, No. I is open so that you can see authentic versions of grand Georgian rooms, from the entrance hall, drawing room, dining room and study to the kitchen and bedroom.

Open: mid Feb–end of Oct: Tue–Sun 10.30–17.00; Nov: Tue–Sun 10.30–16.00, plus two weekends during Dec. Last admission 30 min before closing
Entry: under £5
Tel: 01225 428126
Website: www.bath-preservation-trust.org.uk
Other facilities: gift shop

No. I Royal Crescent

Sally Lunn's House and Museum
North Parade Passage; map D5

Some say that Sally Lunn was a Huguenot refugee who fled to Bath in 1680, carrying with her the recipe for a large, light brioche-type bun which she started to sell from this very house, claimed to be the oldest in Bath. Others think that 'Sally Lunn' might be convenient rhyming slang. Whatever their origin, these rich dough cakes make the base for sweet and savoury meals which you can enjoy from the café/restaurant here. For extra interest, visit the museum in the basement where excavations have revealed occupation as far back as Roman times.

Open: museum open daily; Mon–Sat 10.00–18.00; Sun 11.00–18.00;

restaurant open for lunch, tea and evening meal

Entry to museum: free if eating in restaurant, otherwise a nominal charge
Tel: 01225 461634
Other facilities: gift shop

Sally Lunn's restaurant and museum

LEGENDARY FODDER
You'll notice handsome carved stone acorns adorning many of Bath's buildings, including the houses in The Circus. These mark the legend of Prince Bladud's pigs, who could be enticed from the hot spring water only by acorns, their favourite food.

Theatre Royal
Sawclose; map C4

A pretty, and reputedly haunted, building was first constructed on this site in 1805. The Theatre Royal was rebuilt in 1862/3 after a devastating fire, reopening with a performance of *A Midsummer Night's Dream*, with Ellen Terry playing Titania. Now you can see a range of shows from pre- and post-West End productions to concerts and contemporary plays. There is a restaurant and the theatre's own pub, the Garrick's Head, once the home of Beau Nash. The house on the other side, now Popjoy's restaurant, belonged to his mistress, Juliana. You might also experience one of the many ghosts which include a jasmine-scented grey lady, a phantom doorman and a mysterious butterfly.

Theatre Royal

Open: contact the theatre for performance times
Tel: 01225 448844
Website: www.theatreroyal.org.uk
Disabled access: full to the theatre, but none to the restaurant or pub
Other facilities: restaurant and pub (see left)

Thermae Bath Spa
Hot Bath Street; map C5

For the first time in 25 years people can immerse themselves once more in the natural, hot spring waters of Bath. A multi-million pound grant from the Millennium Commission has enabled the restoration of five historic buildings into a magnificent spa, crowned with an open-air rooftop pool with a view over the city and the surrounding hills. The hot water feeding the bathing pools, whirlpool baths and steam rooms is drawn from the Hetling Spring, the Cross Spring and the King's Spring, the three natural water supplies that deliver more than 1,000,000 litres (250,000 gallons) of water daily. Thermae is able to boast that it is the only place in Britain where you can bathe in natural thermal waters. There are two hot pools, one on the ground floor and the open-air rooftop bath, several steam rooms, massage and treatment rooms, a restaurant and visitor centre. The restored buildings include the Georgian Hot Bath and Cross Bath, while an architecturally acclaimed new glass and stone building completes the construction.

DON'T MISS
A dip in the warm, rooftop pool with its terrace overlooking the city.

Open: daily; 9.00–22.00 (last entry 20.00)
Entry: from £17 depending on time spent in the Spa
Tel: 01225 336789 (enquiries);
01225 331234 (bookings)
Website: www.thermaebathspa.com
Disabled access: full
Other facilities: shop and restaurant

The main spa pool

The rooftop spa pool

Victoria Art Gallery
Bridge Street; map D4

A fine collection of paintings, sculpture and decorative arts. The permanent collection on the first floor includes works by Gainsborough, Turner and Sickert, all of whom lived in Bath for a while. Among the other treasures is a collection of 18th-century glass and more than 150 china dogs. The gallery on the ground floor displays a variety of interesting temporary exhibitions.

Open: Tue–Fri 10.00–17.30, Sat 10.00–17.00, Sun 14.00–17.00
Entry: free
Tel: 01225 477772
Website: www.victoriagal.org.uk
Disabled access: limited
Other facilities: gift shop, free audio-guides explaining major pieces, activities to help children enjoy the collection, workshops and talks

Victoria Art Gallery

William Herschel House
19 New King Street; map B4

Astronomers William and Caroline Herschel lived here while they were building telescopes and observing the night skies. William, who discovered the planet Uranus in 1781, became the first president of the Royal Astronomical Society. His sister Caroline found eight new comets and was the first female scientist to be elected to the Royal Society. The work of both Herschels, who came to Bath from their native Hanover, is acknowledged to have had an impact on modern science and space. Both were accomplished musicians as well as distinguished astronomers.

The house isn't grand, but very interesting, showing not only the work of two talented people but also something of the life of a middle-class household. A new audio-visual display helps put the Herschels' work in perspective.

DON'T MISS
The basement with a kitchen leading directly into the workshop where the Herschels built their telescopes.
The portraits of William and Caroline in the dining room.
The charming formal Georgian town garden with box-lined borders, quince trees and plenty of herbs.

Open: mid Feb–30 Nov: Thu–Tue 14.00–17.00; Sat and Sun 11.00–17.00. Closed Wed
Entry: under £5
Tel: 01225 311342
Website: www.bath-preservation-trust.org.uk
Disabled access: limited

Hedgemead Park (page 57)

BREATHING SPACE

Even in the heart of Bath you're never far from a green space and a shady seat. Everywhere there are sudden views of the green hills beyond. In the city itself you'll find beautifully tended parks and squares with space to enjoy a picnic, read a book or simply to sit and enjoy peace in perfect surroundings.

Sydney Gardens

Parade Gardens; map E4

This city-centre favourite has a smart bandstand and poignant little statue of a violin-playing Mozart, dedicated to Mark Purnell, with the inscription 'Play Mozart in memory of me'. The River Avon flows past and there are good views up to Pulteney Bridge and the weir.

Sydney Gardens

Sydney Gardens, Jane Austen's retreat, lies across the river behind Sydney Place. There Jane would walk from the family lodgings in Sydney Street. The Kennet and Avon Canal cuts through Sydney Gardens and you can stroll along the towpath as far as Bath Spa Station.

Royal Victoria Park

TREAT YOURSELF
If you're feeling flush, hit the heights with a champagne balloon flight from Royal Victoria Park (see page 83).

Henrietta Park;
map E2

Another favourite on the Bathwick side of the river is Henrietta Park, full of meandering paths and ancient trees. Enclosed within the park is a sensory garden full of strongly scented plants and a pretty memorial garden, with a pond, to George V.

Hedgemead Park;
map D1

You'll have to puff your way up The Paragon or Lansdown Road to reach Hedgemead Park, set on a steep hillside. There used to be a vineyard here – and more than 100 houses which collapsed in a landslide in the late 19th century when the area became a public park. You'll find a pretty bandstand and a children's play area.

Green Park;
map A5

At the other end of town is the smaller Green Park on the riverbank, with a children's play area, too.

Queen Square;
map B3–D3

Queen Square in the centre of the city was

designed by architect John Wood who wrote: 'I preferred an inclosed Square to an open one.' The Square is named in honour of Queen Caroline, George II's wife. The central obelisk commemorates a visit by Frederick, Prince of Wales.

Queen Square

Parade Gardens

Royal Victoria Park;
map A2–B2

Bath's largest public open space is the 23-hectare (57-acre) Royal Victoria Park with its botanical gardens. It is not always the most peaceful of parks, hosting many of Bath's summer events, including Bath Festival, concerts and flower shows. Hot-air balloons soar into the sky from here and there is an imaginative children's playground.

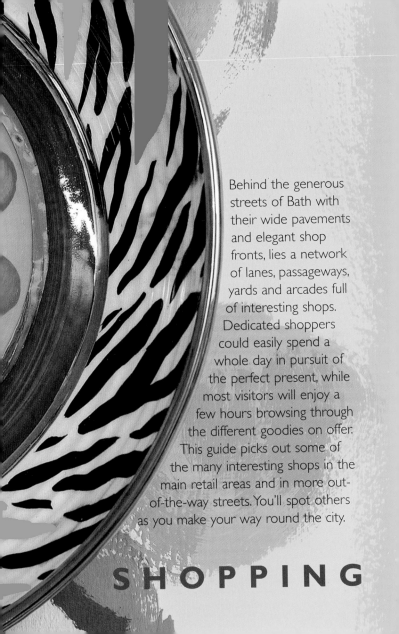

Behind the generous
streets of Bath with
their wide pavements
and elegant shop
fronts, lies a network
of lanes, passageways,
yards and arcades full
of interesting shops.
Dedicated shoppers
could easily spend a
whole day in pursuit of
the perfect present, while
most visitors will enjoy a
few hours browsing through
the different goodies on offer.
This guide picks out some of
the many interesting shops in the
main retail areas and in more out-
of-the-way streets. You'll spot others
as you make your way round the city.

SHOPPING

Opening hours

Most shops open seven days a week, even during the winter. On Sundays opening hours are generally shorter than those of the rest of the week.

High Street shops and department stores

High Street names and chain stores are to be found in the Southgate area, along Stall Street and Union Street and in the Podium Centre off Northgate Street. Nearly half of Bath's shops are independently owned, ensuring an inspiring mix of the new and unusual.

Jolly's of Bath
Milsom Street;
map C3

Bath's shopping heart is in the handsome and fashionable Milsom Street, where in 1831 Mr James Jolly opened the Bath Emporium. Jolly's of Bath, the world's oldest department store, still dominates the street with its imposing granite, bronze and mahogany shop front which was added in 1879. It now belongs to The House of Fraser and still offers shoppers an excellent choice of goods in an elegant building.

Clothes shops
Children's and teens'
Abbey Gate Street;
map D5

There is plenty of choice at the Golden Cot, which has been supplying Bath's babies with prams and pushchairs and clothes for more than 40 years.

Northumberland Place;
map D4

This is one of Bath's narrow passages where you'll find Just Add Water, full of a fabulous range of trendy clothes for children and young people at prices that won't break the bank.

Walcot Street;
map D1–D3

This street is full of exciting shops, including the colourful Walcot Woollies with terrific baby and kids' wear. They stock clothes such as bright fleeces and dungarees, boots and strawberry hats and organic cotton clobber for babies. There are plenty of lovely souvenirs for grown-ups too.

Walcot Woollies

THE NOWHERE PLACE

Art and crafts area Walcot Street was once 'wiped out' by cartographers who left the whole street off a new map of Bath. Now the 'Nation Day' street party, held once a year during the annual Fringe Festival, celebrates that error which encouraged Walcot Street residents to think of themselves as a nation apart.

Square

Designer clothes
Shires Yard; map C3

Connecting Milsom Street and Broad Street is the splendid Shires Yard where Walter Wiltshire, an 18th-century Mayor of Bath, kept horses for his carting business. The horses are long gone, replaced by clothes shops such as the excellent Square, which stocks classic labels alongside styles by avant-garde designers. It is not far to go to complete your outfit next door at Square Shoes and Bags. Annabel Harrison and Italian Connection and Charles Ashley Shoes are all here, along with other boutiques.

Broad Street and Green Street; map D3

Take the Shires Yard passageway into Broad Street where Red Eye sells young labels such as Ben Sherman and Urban Stone. Not too far away in Green Street, Maze sells its own label and designer clothes for both men and women.

Margaret's Buildings; map B2

A little way out of the main shopping centre,

near Royal Crescent, is Margaret's Buildings, where you can splash out on a top designer outfit at classy JAQ, or buy a beautiful bag from Bath designer Liz Cox.

Liz Cox

Hats
Walcot Street; map D3

The lower end of Walcot Street is where you'll find the perfect hat – in The British Hatter, a tiny shop crammed full of classy, trendy, classic and wacky headgear. Whatever titfer you're after, this must be the place.

The British Hatter

Hungerford Bazaar
Pulteney Bridge; map D3

It's hard not to be tempted inside the uniquely situated Hungerford Bazaar, with its windows of very wearable women's clothes.

Retro
Walcot Street; map D1–D3

If you're stuck in a time warp or just think things look better the second time around, go to Jack and Danny's, a treasure house of retro gear at the top end of the street.

Shoes
New Bond Street Place and Old Bond Street; map C3–D3

Shoon is an old Scottish word for shoes and Silvershoon of New Bond Street Place is full of – yes – shoes for both men and women. They've taken things a bit further in Old Bond Street where Shoon sells not only sporty and outdoor gear, but also accessories for men and women, and unrelated, but practical and classy, goods. There's a second-floor café, where you can buy coffee, smoothies, crois-sants and breakfasty food.

IF THE HAT FITS...
Jane Austen's scheming
Isabella Thorpe in *Northanger
Abbey* loved window shop-
ping in Milsom Street. 'I saw
the prettiest hat you can
imagine,' she exclaimed. 'I
quite longed for it.'

The British Hatter

Fishworks (page 64)

The Fine Cheese Co.

Food shops
Bread
**Argyle Street;
map D3**
Bread more tempting than most is sold at Phipps Bakery. They have another outlet in George Street.

**Cheesemongers
Quiet Street, Walcot
Street; map C3
and D3**
Paxton and Whitfield have been cheesemongers for more than 200 years. The huge variety includes a locally made, soft cheese. Not established so long, but with a glowing and growing recommendation, is

Ann-Marie Dyas' The Fine Cheese Co. The choice is huge and you won't be able to go in without buying a lot more than you intended. They do all

sorts of gourmet goodies, delicious sandwiches, good bread and they have a seating area as well where you can enjoy coffee or lunch.

QUIET MAN OF BATH
Architect John Wood (1704–54) designed much of Bath that we see today. He was anxious, so the story goes, for the streets to be given names, so that he could order the carving of the stones. Insisting once more that the corporation made up its collective mind, he got his answer. 'Quiet, John Wood!' shouted the chairman, finally losing patience.

Wood left the room and ordered three stones to be carved: Quiet Street, John Street and Wood Street.

Fish
Green Street; map D3
Foodies should head for Green Street where they'll find Fishworks – a traditional fishmongers fronting an award-winning fish restaurant and cookery school.

The Sausage Shop

The Sausage Shop
Green Street; map D3
Right next door is The Sausage Shop with more than 30 different types of banger made daily – from Toulouse sausage to Champion Aldridge and Merguez.

Gifts
The Corridor; map D4
You can almost follow your nose to Lotus Emporium with its handmade aromatherapy gifts, soaps and incense.

Northumberland Place; map D4
Nothing could be easier than buying a present for a cat lover – just head for Cat Out of the Bag, where anything feline goes.

Queen Street; map C3–C4
Here is Firebird, full of colourful Russian crafts, and the stylish Harington Glass, which sells ornamental and practical pieces from individual glass makers.

Union Passage; map D4
In narrow Union Passage is The Silver Shop of Bath, good for gift-hunters.

Upper Borough Walls; map C4
List-makers and writers will love Papyrus with its pens, handmade papers, notebooks and albums.

Walcot Street; map D2
You won't find a more colourful present than the bright and beautiful pots, bowls, cups and mugs made by Mary Rose Young and sold at her Walcot Street shop, which is looked after by her charming mother.

Museum shops
Some of the most interesting reminders of your time in Bath are to be found at the museum gift shops (see pages 33–55). The Roman Baths (map D4) sells a range of gifts including replicas of the Gorgon's Head.
The Museum of Costume (map C2) has a gift shop and costume bookshop.
Gifts relating to Jane Austen and the Georgian period can be found at the Jane Austen Centre (map C3) and No. 1 Royal Crescent (map A1).
The Victoria Art Gallery (map D4) sells cards, gifts and items related to the

changing exhibitions.
The Holburne Museum
(map F2) and the Bath
Industrial Heritage Centre
(map C1) both have
shops, as does the
Museum of East Asian Art
(map C2), where you'll
find gifts with a difference.
Interesting books can be
bought at The Building of
Bath Museum shop (map
D1) and at the bookshop
in Bath Abbey (map D4).

Mary Rose Young

Homes and gardens
Antiques
There are plenty of
antiques shops scattered
around Bath but dedi-
cated hunters make a
beeline for the Lansdown
Road and London Road
area (map C1–D1)
and the Bartlett Street
Antiques Centre, which
is behind George Street
(map C2).

Rossiters

The Paragon; map D1
The Bath Antiques Centre
and Paragon Antiques
Market sit side by side.

Walcot Street;
map D2
The famous Walcot Street
Reclamation Yard has
attracted other similar
business, so a hunt for
unusual items for homes

and gardens starts
here. Nearby is Abbey
Furniture, which sells
Victorian bits and pieces
for the garden.

Everything for the home
Broad Street; map D4
Broad Street (which isn't)
is where you'll find the
rambling and splendid

Rossiters with four floors
dedicated to goods for
the home, from teaspoons
to sleigh beds, from fruit
bowls to kitchen ranges.
Just up the road is
Susannah, a shop full of
lovely items for adding
extra touches to most
rooms in the house.
Across the road, Mandarin

sells handmade tiles and stone for floors and walls, while The Knob Connection will help you open doors and other things, too.

Garden store
Quiet Street; map C3
The hugely popular London garden shop, RK Alliston, chose this street for its first and only branch outside the capital

and, if you wonder why a garden store does well in a city, go and take a look.

Indian and fair-trade crafts
New Bond Street Place; map D3
The huge market area in Delhi is called Chandni Chowk; check out the Bath branch of Chandni Chowk in New Bond Street Place for Indian

rugs, cushions, bedspreads and an assortment of imported household goods. And this is where you'll find Tumi, a fair-trade shop with traditional and contemporary crafts from Latin America.

The Linen Press
Margaret's Buildings; map B2
At the other end of town, in Margaret's Buildings, The Linen Press sells luxury bedroom and bathroom accessories. Good for wedding presents.

Jewellery
Northumberland Place; map D4
Goldsmith Nicholas Wylde will make a piece of jewellery to order or you can choose from the lovely pieces on display, including many of his own designs. Here you'll also find Justice, a showcase for British jewellery designers where you'll find striking and original bangles, bracelets, rings, brooches, earrings and necklaces.

Queen Street and Quiet Street; map C3
Queen Street is home to the Gold and Silver Studio where pieces are made on

RK Alliston

the premises and laid out in the first-floor gallery. Bloomsbury Jewellery, in next door Quiet Street, has lovely contemporary work, too.

Union Passage; map D4
Just a step away is The Silver Shop, with a huge collection of well-displayed silver jewellery on two floors.

Other specialist shops
Art galleries
Brock Street; map B2
The Rooksmoor Gallery has bang-up-to-the-minute paintings and ceramics from new artists.

Chapel Row; map B4
Hitchcocks' is a magnet for collectors of automata and mechanical toys.

George Street; map C3/C2
The Rosta Gallery deals in contemporary art.

Margaret's Buildings; map B2
In the upper part of Bath is the Anthony Hepworth Gallery selling fine 20th-century work.

Quiet Street; map C3
The Adam Gallery has

Hitchcocks' Gallery

work by 20th-century artists, such as Piper, Nash and Moore, and the St Ives School.

Dolls' houses
Broad Street; map D4
Caroline Nevill Miniatures sells tiny handmade furnishings and fittings for dolls' houses, as well as the houses themselves.

Flowers and memorabilia
Pulteney Bridge; map D3
Robert Adams' famous shop-lined Pulteney Bridge, with its three graceful arches, echoes the older Rialto Bridge in Venice. Pulteney Bridge Flowers flourishes here, while across the road is

Nauticalia, selling a range of maritime memorabilia.

Old and rare books
Manvers Street; map E6
George Bayntun and George Gregory has been established here for more than 100 years, selling old and rare books and antique prints.

Toys
Walcot Street; map D2
Who can resist a toyshop? And Tridias is everything a toyshop should be. It's big and bright with plenty of proper toys and will keep most grown-ups happily occupied for just as long as the kids.

Guildhall Market

Travel goods
Northumberland Place;
map D4
Long-established Rickards
of Bath have travel all
wrapped up with bags,
briefcases, rucksacks, suit-
cases, purses and wallets
for every journey.

Markets
Antique market
Everyone looks forward
to the Saturday antiques
market in Walcot Street
(map D2).

Arts and crafts market
Green Park Station
(map A4)
This old station is home to
an arts and crafts market
from Wed–Sat each week.

Farmers' markets
There are also two farm-
ers' markets each month
at the old railway station.

Guildhall Market
The Guildhall Market in
the High Street (map D4)
is a superstore in its own
right with 25 shops selling
a variety of goods from
coffee and tea to bread,
meat, hardware, antiques,
books and flowers. You
can get your hair cut at
the barber's shop and buy
breakfast at the café.

The Fine Cheese Co. (page 63)

'Water is best' runs the inscription over the Pump Room door and round the charming little Rebecca Fountain behind the Abbey, but you don't have to take that too seriously. Of course you should try the spring water – at 50p a glass from the Pump Room fountain, it's an experience not to be missed. But Bath, with some of the bes cafés, coffee shops, bistros, pubs and restaurants in the country, has a lot more to offer. If it's British food you're after, look in the world-class section of the restaurants.

EATING AN
DRINKING

Demuth's Restaurant (page 76)

Shires Yard

CAFES

You'll find all the old familiar names: Starbucks and Costa Coffee are here in Bath along with plenty of in-store coffee shops.

Around the Roman Baths

It's almost obligatory to take coffee and a sugary Bath bun in the elegant Georgian Pump Room, to the civilized strains of the musical trio. And you ought to visit nearby Sally Lunn's in North Parade Passage (map D5) to try the eponymous brioche-type bun.

Chocoholics will rejoice to find Café Cadbury at

23 Union Street (map C4/D4), where they do a mean cup of chocolate and plenty of chocolate goodies to eat. Or there's Café Shoon on the second floor of the shop with the same name in Old Bond Street (map C3–C4) – good coffee, smoothies and breakfast-type food.

Bartlett Road; map C2

Lovejoys is the tongue-in-cheek name of the café at the Antiques Centre.

Kingsmead Square; map C4

The Jazz Café is good if you are in this area.

Shires Yard; map C3

Here you'll get a little taste of France at Café Rene. Nearby is Le Parisien, good for breakfast and light lunches.

Pulteney Bridge; map D3

Try the Pulteney Bridge Café or venture right up to the end of Pulteney Street to take refreshment at the award-winning teahouse in the grounds of the Holburne Museum at Sydney Place.

Walcot Street; map D2

Doolallys, the most colourful café you'll visit, is well worth the shoe leather to reach it.

RESTAURANTS

You're spoilt for choice with restaurants, brasseries and bistros for lunch or dinner. The list below is not exhaustive but will give an idea of what's on offer.

American

The Firehouse Rotisserie
2 John Street; map C3
Californian mix of flame-roasted meat, gourmet pizzas and vegetarian.
Tel: 01225 482070

Las Iguanas
12 Seven Dials, Sawclose; map C4
Young and exciting atmosphere in this lively Latin American café-bar.
Tel: 01225 336666

Doolallys (page 71)

Brasseries, bistros and wine bars

Bathtub Bistro
2 Grove Street; map D3
Varied menu, with a good choice of several vegetarian dishes.
Tel: 01225 460593

Café Retro
York Street; map D4
Laid back café and restaurant that is popular with everyone – students, business people and shoppers alike.
Tel: 01225 339347

Café Retro

Clarkes Wine Bar and Restaurant
7 Argyle Street; map D3
Stylish wine bar at street level and luxurious downstairs restaurant. Good value for money.
Tel: 01225 444440

Fitzroys Brasserie
Dukes Hotel, Great Pulteney Street; map E3
Fine food from two-Michelin-star chef Martin Blunos, served in a relaxed atmosphere.
Tel: 01225 787960

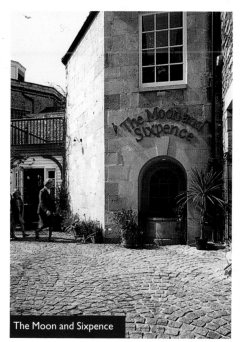

The Moon and Sixpence

Green Park Brasserie and Bar
Green Park Station; map A4–B4
Food with a French influence in a magnificent old Victorian station.
Tel: 01225 338565

Ha! Ha! Bar and Canteen
Beehive Yard, Walcot Street; map D2
Good fusion food in brand new setting.
Tel: 01225 421200

The Moon and Sixpence
6a Broad Street; map D3
Informal self-service downstairs, waitress-service restaurant above; uses fresh local produce.
Tel: 01225 460962

Popjoys
Sawclose; map C4
Modern British food served in a house with a history next to the Theatre Royal.
Tel: 01225 465350

Raphaels
Upper Borough Walls; map C4–D4
Popular restaurant open all day for coffee, a glass of wine or a relaxed meal.
Tel: 01225 480042

Tilleys
3 North Parade Passage; map D5
You can have it all – they'll even serve two or more starter-size portions of whatever you fancy.
Tel: 01225 484200

The Walrus and the Carpenter
28 Barton Street; map C4
Another Bath favourite serving wonderful salads, burgers and veggie food.
Tel: 01225 314864

The Wife of Bath
Pierrepont Street; map D5
Attractive bistro serving good steaks, casseroles, fresh fish and veggie food.
Tel: 01225 461745

Woods Brasserie and Restaurant
9–12 Alfred Street; map C2
Much-loved and long-established eaterie serving modern English food with a French influence.
Tel: 01225 314812

Woods Brasserie and Restaurant
(page 73)

Chinese
Peking Chinese
Restaurant
1–2 New Street,
Kingsmead Square;
map C4
Peking, Cantonese and
Szechuan cooking –
seafood a speciality.
Tel: 01225
466377/461750

Xian Restaurant
28 Charles Street; map B4
Pretty restaurant with

reputation for good
regional cooking that's
freshly prepared.
Tel: 01225 424917

French
Le Beaujolais
5 Chapel Row, Queen
Square; map B3
Bath's favourite French
restaurant. Menus range
from good provincial
cooking to haute cuisine.
Wonderful wines.
Tel: 01225 423417

Le Beaujolais

Bistro Papillon
Margaret's Buildings;
map B2
Mediterranean colour
scheme and good bistro-
style cooking.
Tel: 01225 310064

No. 5 Restaurant
Argyle Street;
map D3
Popular restaurant serving
excellent food at reason-
able prices.
Tel: 01225 444499

Indian
Bengal Brasserie
Milsom Street; map C3
Cosy and popular;
traditional Indian food at
reasonable prices.
Tel: 01225 447906

The Eastern Eye
8a Quiet Street; map C3
Food guides vote this one

The Eastern Eye

No. 5 Restaurant

of the best Indian restaurants in the country. And
you eat in magnificent
Georgian surroundings.
Tel: 01225 422323

Pria Balti
Argyle Street;
map D3
Indian food at very
reasonable prices.
Tel: 01225 462323

Rajpoot
4 Argyle Street;
map D3
Another award-winning
eatery, not far from
Pulteney Bridge.
Tel: 01225 466833

Italian
Café Uno
The Empire, Grand
Parade; map D4

Classic Italian food, accom-
panied by good views
over Pulteney Weir.
Tel: 01225 461140

Il Bottelinos
5 Bladud Buildings, The
Paragon; map D1–D2
Popular family-run restau-
rant; delicious pizzas.
Tel: 01225 464861

Martini Restaurant
8–9 George Street;
map C3
Authenic Italian food;
there is also a good vegetarian choice, including
stone-baked pizzas.
Tel: 01225 460818

Pasta Galore
Barton Street; map C4
Good Italian food, both
traditional and modern.
Tel: 01225 463861

Japanese
Sakura
(at the Windsor Hotel)
Great Pulteney Street;
map E3–F3
They'll guide you through
an authentic menu in a
dining room overlooking a
traditional Japanese
garden. Three set menus
offer choices, including
shabu shabu, sukiyaki and
seafood nabe.
Tel: 01225 422100

Martini Restaurant
(page 75)

Sukhothai
Walcot Street; map
D1–D3
Popular, with good,
reasonably priced food in
cosy atmosphere.
Tel: 01225 462463

Yum Yum Thai
17 Kingsmead Square;
map C4
Café atmosphere, good-
value Thai food with
plenty of vegetarian
choice. Take-away too.
Tel: 01225 445253

Vegetarian
Demuth's Restaurant
2 North Parade Passage;
map D5
Imaginative food for vege-
tarians and vegans. They
also run a cookery school.
Tel: 01225 446059

Seafood
Fishworks Seafood Cafe
6 Green Street;
map D3
A brimming fishmonger's
counter fronts a restau-
rant selling the most
wonderful seafood.
Tel: 01225 488707

Loch Fyne Restaurant
Milsom Street; map C3
Stylish restaurant with
plenty of fishy choices.
Tel: 01225 750120

Thai and Asian:
F.East
High Street; map D4
Pan-Asian restaurant.
Order several portions of
delicious south-east Asian
dishes to share.
Tel: 01225 333500

Mai Thai
6 Pierrepont Street;
map E5
Reliable Thai menu in old
Georgian house.
Tel: 01225 445557

World-class cooking
Bath Priory Hotel
restaurant
Weston Road
Michelin-starred restau-
rant offering classic food
in very comfortable
surroundings.
Tel: 01225 331922

Blinis Restaurant
Argyle Street; map
D3–E3
Café bar and restaurant
with food from Martin

Moody Goose

Blunos who holds two Michelin stars. Dining room with views over the Avon and Pulteney Weir. Tel: 01225 422510

**The Hole in the Wall
16 George Street;
map C2**
Probably the best-known Bath restaurant. Holds a

The Hole in the Wall

Michelin Bib Gourmande and serves modern British food with flair. Tel: 01225 425242

**Moody Goose
7a Kingsmead Square;
map C4**
A Michelin star is held by this charming restaurant which places strong emphasis on fresh local produce simply prepared. Tel: 01225 466688

**Olive Tree Restaurant
Russel Street; map C1**
The Olive Tree, at the Queensberry Hotel, serves contemporary English food with a

Mediterranean influence. Tel: 01225 447928

The Boater
(page 79)

TASTES OF BATH

Bath buns are
delicious spiced
and fruited sugary
concoctions,
served plain or
toasted with
butter. You'll also
find the famous
Bath Oliver
biscuit, served
with top people's
cheese. The recipe
was devised by
Bath physician
Dr William Oliver,
co-founder of the
Royal Mineral
Water Hospital, to
help his patients
curb their weight.

The Porter

PUBS

The Bell, 103 Walcot Street; map D1–D3
Famed for its incredible garden and live music.

The Bathwick Boatman, Forester Road, Bathwick
Pub/restaurant, with car park. This pub also serves good food.

The Boater, 9 Argyle Street; map D3
Fun pub, popular with students, with garden overlooking the river.

The Chequers Inn, River Street
Traditional pub serving good food.

Crystal Palace, Abbey Green; map D5
Very pretty and popular pub that also serves excellent food.

Garrick's Head, Sawclose; map C4
Theatre pub with convivial atmosphere and good food, too.

King's Arms, Monmouth Place; map B3
Lots of loud music and a lively atmosphere.

Old Green Tree, Green Street; map C3–D3
Peaceful pub in city centre with an excellent lunchtime menu.

The Porter, George Street; map C2
Bath's only vegetarian pub.

The Pulteney Arms, 37 Daniel Street; map F2
Pub that proudly preserves many of its old features.

The Star Inn, The Paragon; map D1–D2
Real old pubby feel – they still serve Bass from a jug.

Crystal Palace

AN EVENING OUT

Don't plan any early nights on your visit to Bath – you'll miss too much.

Comedy walk

Top of the evening pops seems to be the anarchic Bizarre Bath comedy walk, established well over 10 years ago and a much-loved, if somewhat eccentric, event. All you have to do is meet your guides at 20.00 outside the Huntsman Inn in North Parade (map E4). You hand over £5 and are then treated to 90 minutes of comedy and moments of sheer lunacy as you stroll round the streets. The walk happens every evening during the summer, from 1 April to the end of September. No need to book but, if you want more information, telephone 01225 335124.

Roman Baths

You've seen the Roman Baths (map D4) in daylight – but they're very romantic by torchlight too. During July and August you can spend an evening wandering round this 2,000-year-old marvel. Last admission is 21.00. More information on 01225 477785.

Theatre Royal

A night at the theatre is always a treat, especially at such a pretty playhouse as the Theatre Royal in Sawclose (map C4). You can eat at the theatre's own restaurant, The Vaults, or take a drink at the Garrick's Head, also attached. Plenty of nearby restaurants (see pages 71–77) do pre- or post-theatre suppers. Telephone 01225 448844 for box office information.

Festivals

If you plan your visit to Bath during one of the major festivals you're spoilt for choice. The

International Music Festival during the last two weeks in May each year sees world-class musicians performing at various venues throughout the city, while the Literature Festival happens in early March. Telephone 01225 463362 for details.

Concerts

Throughout the year there are concerts at the Abbey (map D4) and the Assembly Rooms (map C2), while the Bath Mozartfest is held in early November (details of Mozartfest on 01225 429750).

Film

Latest films are shown at the ABC Beau Nash or the Robins Cinema, both near the Theatre Royal, as is the Little Theatre which is now a cinema, showing art-house and classic foreign movies.

Eating out

It would take a lot of time and a voracious appetite to eat your way round Bath but you can spend some very enjoyable evenings trying out several of the many different restaurants and pubs (see pages 70–79).

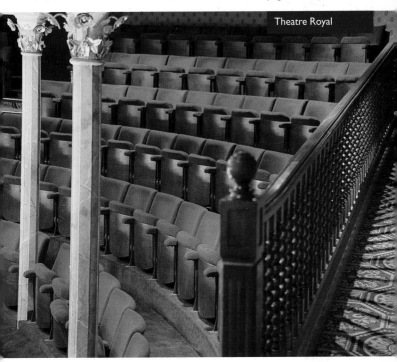

Theatre Royal

On the water

The River Avon and the Kennet and Avon Canal can both be explored by boat. The return trip lasts an hour or you can hop off for lunch and come back on a later boat. From April to the end of September you can simply turn up at Pulteney Weir (reached by steps at the Argyle Street end of Pulteney Bridge, map D3) and take a river cruise to Bathampton. During February, March, October and November the trips run at weekends only. Telephone 01225 466407 for details.

You can charter the *John Rennie* for special parties or trips. She leaves from Sydney Wharf, Bathwick Hill and takes up to 54 people. Telephone 01225 447276 for information.

For an environmentally-friendly electric boat trip from Pulteney Weir, contact the Small Green Boat company on 01225 460831.

If you like to do-it-yourself, hire a punt or canoe from the Bath Boating Station. Details on 01225 466407.

TOURS AND TRIPS

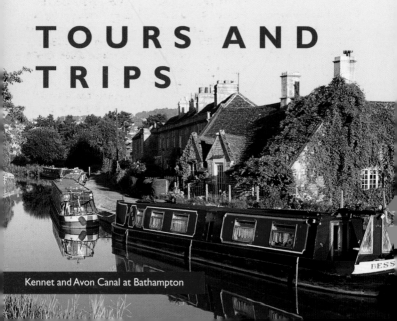

Kennet and Avon Canal at Bathampton

On foot

Bath is a small city and it's easy to see a lot on foot. There are many guided walks including the daily, free, two-hour exploration with the Mayor of Bath's Corps of Honorary Guides. They meet at the Pump Room, Abbey Church Yard (map D4) starting at 10.30 and 14.00 on Sunday to Friday, and at 10.30 only on Saturday. From May to the end of September, there is an extra walk on Tuesday, Friday and Saturday starting at 19.00. Telephone 01225 4777411.

Try the hilarious Bizarre Bath evening walk (see page 80) from April to September. Telephone 01225 335124.

Don't stray from the rest of the party during the Ghost Walks of Bath when

Pulteney Bridge

you'll hear the sad stories of 30 hapless wraiths. Meet at 20.00 at the Garrick's Head pub (map C4) at 20.00 on Monday to Saturday from April to the end of October; walks are on Friday only between November and the end of March. Telephone 01225 463618.

The Jane Austen Walk leaves daily at 13.30 during July and August from KC Change in the Abbey Church Yard (map D4). You can join it on Saturdays and Sundays and public holidays during the rest of the year. Tel: 01225 4433000

By bus

Open-top bus tours are a great feature of city life and you can get on and off to see the best of Bath. Telephone 09068 360394.

By balloon

If you've seen Bath from every other angle you might like to soar up, up and away, with a glass of champagne in one hand. Several balloon companies fly from Royal Victoria Park. It will set you back around £135, but it's a unique experience.
Bath Balloon Flights: 01225 466888.
Heritage Balloons: 01225 318747.

> **TREAT YOURSELF**
> Board a river cruiser at Pulteney Weir (map E4) and enjoy a trip along the river to Bathampton.

Somerset Place

WHAT'S ON

Throughout the year major festivals and international events are highlights on a calendar already offering plenty of diversion and entertainment. Bath's Georgian public rooms, including the Pump Room, the Assembly Rooms and the Guildhall, are the perfect venues for many of the more formal events, while the Abbey plays host to concerts, especially around Christmas time. Royal Victoria Park, with the grand sweep of Royal Crescent behind, is the setting for flower shows, balloon fiestas, and any celebrations that require a large open space.

Balloon fiesta

Art and music

Bath's literary giant, Jane Austen, has a festival all to herself, while Mozart enthusiasts celebrate the master's music over a ten-day stretch and Shakespeare buffs enjoy a two-week feast during March. Perhaps the best known of all the Bath celebrations is the two-week International Music Festival in May and June, when world-class musicians can be seen and heard at various venues around the city.

Light show

Many people visit during July and August simply to see the world-renowned Roman Baths by torch light as closing time moves, for these two months only, to the later time of 22.00.

Sport

Cricket is celebrated in an annual June festival while a half-marathon is run through Bath in March. Bath Rugby Club play regularly from September to April at the Recreation

Fringe festival

Fireworks

Ground; map E4.
Telephone 09068 884554
for recorded information.

Christmas market

The newest event is the
very popular continental-
style Christmas market,
held in the heart of the
city near the Abbey.

Festivals and major events

Full information on these
annual events is available
from the Tourist
Information Centre;
tel: 01225 477101.

March

Literature Festival, various
venues; tel: 01225 463362
Shakespeare Festival,
Theatre Royal;
tel: 01225 448844
Bath Half-Marathon;
tel: 01225 471282

April

Easter Candlelit Concert,
the Assembly Rooms;
tel: 01225 463362

May

Spring Flower Show,
Royal Victoria Park;
tel: 01225 482624

May/June

International Music
Festival, various venues;
tel: 01225 463362
Bath Fringe Festival,
various venues;
tel: 01225 463362

June

Somerset Country
Cricket Festival,
Recreation Ground;
tel: 01823 272946

July

Roman Baths by Torchlight;
tel: 01225 477785

July/Aug

International Guitar
Festival, various venues;
tel: 01225 463362

August

Roman Baths by
Torchlight
tel: 01225 477785

September

Jane Austen Festival;
tel: 01225 443000

October

Bath Film Festival;
tel: 01225 401149

November

Fireworks display,
Recreation Ground;
tel: 01225 423271
Bath Mozartfest, various
venues; tel: 01225 429750
Heritage Open Week,
various venues throughout
the city during school half-
term week;
tel: 01225 477785

Nov/Dec

Christmas at Claverton,
The American Museum;
tel: 01225 460503
Bath Christmas Market,
Kingston Parade/Abbey
Green; tel 01225 477725

December

Christmas music in various
venues; tel: 01225 463362

A city break with children in tow needn't be a daunting experience. Bath's parks are large and well spread round the city. Several are equipped with children's playgrounds. Most of the major attractions (see pages 32–55) have children's activities and workshops, while many restaurants welcome youngsters.

BATH FOR KIDS

Playgrounds

Children of all ages will enjoy a visit to Bath's largest open space, the 23-hectare (57-acre) Royal Victoria Park where there is a large and imaginative adventure playground. In high season a bouncy castle and merry-go-round are installed, and there's plenty of space for ball games. Other parks with children's play areas include Sydney Gardens, Hedgemead Park (map D1) and Green Park (map A5).

Amazing maze

Young children will enjoy solving the riddle of Beazer Maze (map E4), a ground maze next to the river with a central mosaic, made of 92,000 marble tesserae, recalling the fearsome Gorgon's head which once hung in the Roman temple by the ancient Baths.

Fun on the river

Messing around on the water is always fun. You can embark on a river trip (see page 82), or paddle your own canoe or punt, which you can hire from the Bath Boating Station (see page 82).

Beazer Maze

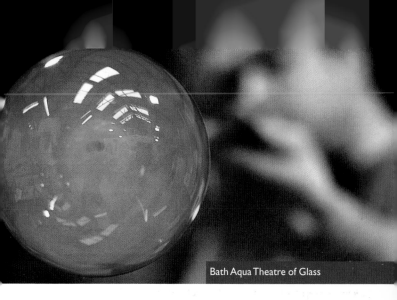

Bath Aqua Theatre of Glass

Spooky and Bizarre walks

A real treat for older kids is the Ghost Walks of Bath (see page 83). Starting at one of Bath's most haunted buildings, the Garrick's Head pub, next to the Theatre Royal, the two-hour trek visits the known abodes of at least 30 ghosts – and it's spooky enough to thrill even the most sophisti-cated teenagers. They'll also enjoy the Bizarre Bath walk (see page 80).

Museums

Children cannot fail to enjoy the Roman Baths (page 49). Award-winning audioguides ensure they get the most out of this unique complex. Regular children's events are held at the American Museum at Claverton Manor (see page 33). Telephone 01225 460503 for details. Other museums that have particularly good chil-dren's activities or exhibits are the Bath Aqua Theatre of Glass (see page 36), the Bath Industrial Heritage Centre (see page 37), Bath Postal Museum (see page 38), the Museum of East Asian Art (see page 42) and the Victoria Art Gallery (see page 54).

Bath balloon fiesta

OUT OF TOWN

There's plenty to see and do in Bath itself, but if you feel like a trip out of town, you'll find lovely countryside and plenty of interesting places to visit. Just a little way out of Bath are the American Museum at Claverton Manor (page 33), Beckford's Tower and Museum (page 38) and Prior Park (page 44). Here are some places that are a little further afield.

Bowood
18 miles east of Bath, near Calne; A4 from Chippenham towards Calne

This traditional English country house is open from spring to mid autumn. The house, with its lovely garden, is worth a visit and you'll enjoy the grand park, laid out by Lancelot 'Capability' Brown. An adventure playground keeps youngsters occupied.
Tel: 01249 812102 for information

Castle Combe
12 miles north-east of Bath; A420 from Chippenham, then B4039

Castle Combe is reckoned by some to be England's prettiest village. It's set deep in a wooded valley with the ruins of the Norman castle on the hills above. There's a 14th-century pub, too.

Cheddar Caves and Gorge
about 20 miles south-west of Bath; A39 to Wells

Cheddar Caves are stupendous, natural, cathedral-like caves, with tunnels and passages that have been hollowed out of the earth since the Ice Age.

Castle Combe

Lacock

The Peto Garden

Our ancestors were living in these caves 9,000 years ago – and had done so for 40,000 years. If you don't do caves, there's always Britain's biggest gorge to marvel at and a signposted scenic five-kilometre (three-mile) walk across breathtaking countryside. Tel: 01934 742343 for information

Dyrham Park is owned by The National Trust. Built around 1700, the magnificent limestone mansion is furnished with Dutch, English and American treasures. Weather permitting, you can see across the Bristol Channel to Wales from the park. Tel: 0117 9 372501 for information

Lacock, too, is very pretty. You can see the Fox Talbot Museum, named for the father of modern photography, and Lacock Abbey. Lacock is much in demand by film-makers – it has featured in *Pride and Prejudice, Emma, Moll Flanders* – as well as *Harry Potter.*

Dyrham Park
8 miles north of Bath;
A46 to near Dyrham

Lacock
15 miles east of Bath;
A4, then A350

The Peto Garden
6 miles south-east of Bath, near Bradford-on-Avon; B3109 going south from Bradford-on-Avon
The Peto Garden at Iford Manor was built by Harold Peto just over 100 years ago. The unique, newly restored terraced garden is full of interesting Italianate architectural detail. Look for the cloisters, the loggia and the Great Terrace. Tel: 01225 863146

THANKSGIVING – AND THE REST
Each year in late November and the first half of December, the American Museum at Claverton celebrates Christmas – American style. Special Christmas gifts, crafts and books are on sale and the tea-room features all sorts of treats from across the water.

WHERE TO STAY

From very grand to cosy, four poster beds to farmhouse, sophisticated to rural, Bath's accommodation comes with style. The Tourist Information Centre (see page 94) has a complete list of hotels, guest houses, bed and breakfast, pubs, self-catering cottages and apartments, and caravan and camping sites. The list below will give you an idea of the range on offer. Best to check facilities and prices before booking.

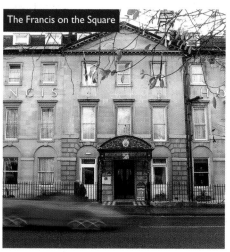

The Francis on the Square

Prices

The £ symbols are an approximate guide for comparing the prices charged, which range from about £25 to over £100 per person per night.

Bath Spa Hotel
Sydney Road, Bath

This Georgian building in 3 hectares (7 acres) of beautiful grounds over-looks the city. It has 102 bedrooms and two restaurants.
Tel: 0870 400 8222
Website:
www.bathspahotel.com
£££

Lucknam Park
Colerne, Chippenham

This Palladian mansion, 6 miles from the city, is set in 200 hectares (500 acres) of parkland. In addition to 41 luxury bedrooms, the hotel has an award-winning restaurant, and a spa.
Tel: 01225 742777
Website:
www.lucknampark.co.uk
£££

The Francis on the Square
Queen Square, Bath; map C3
This 95-bedroom hotel has a splendid location on one side of John Wood's elegant square.
Tel: 0870 400 8223
Website: www.heritage-hotels.com
££

Duke's Hotel
Great Pulteney Street, Bath; map E3–F3
This Palladian-style mansion is just a five-minute walk from the city centre. It has 18 bedrooms and a brasserie-style restaurant overseen by Martin Blunos, a two-star Michelin chef.
Tel: 01225 787960
Website: www.dukesbath.co.uk
££

Harington's Hotel
8–10 Queen Street, Bath; map C3
This small town-house hotel has 13 bedrooms and is in one of Bath's picturesque, cobbled shopping streets in the centre of the city.
Tel: 01225 461728
Website: www.HaringtonsHotel.co.uk
£

The Ayrlington
24/25 Pulteney Road, Bath; map F3–F6
This award-winning 12-bedroom bed-and-breakfast hotel is a Victorian house, built of Bath stone.
Tel: 01225 425495
Website: www.ayrlington.com
£

Paradise House
86–88 Holloway, Bath
This award-winning, small bed-and-breakfast hotel is in a quiet cul-de-sac overlooking the city, and 10 minutes walk from the city centre. It has 11 bedrooms and large, walled gardens.
Tel: 01225 317723
Website: www.paradise-house.co.uk
£

Grey Lodge
Summer Lane, Combe Down, Bath
This mid-Victorian family home in a beautiful garden has only three bedrooms. It is five minutes drive from the city. Bed and breakfast.
Tel: 01225 832069
Website: www.visitbath.co.uk
£

The Beeches Farmhouse
Holt Road, Bradford-on-Avon
They say you can collect your own (free range) eggs for breakfast here if you like. There are just three bedrooms in this 18th-century farmhouse, a few miles from Bath.
Tel: 01225 863475
Website: www.beeches-farmhouse.co.uk
£

Pennsylvania Farm
Newton St Loe, Bath
This is a farmhouse bed and breakfast just 4 miles from Bath, where they're happy to cook evening meals if you ask first. Self-catering cottage as well.
Tel: 01225 314912
Website: www.pensylvaniafarm.co.uk
£

Harington's Hotel

USEFUL INFORMATION

TOURIST INFORMATION

Tourist Information Centre
Abbey Chambers,
Bath BA1 1LY; map D4
Extensive range of services, including accommodation booking, travel and events information.
Open: daily;
1 Oct–30 Apr:
Mon–Sat 9.30–17.00;
Sun 10–16.00;
1 May–30 Sep:
Mon–Sat 09.30–18.00;
Sun 10.00–16.00
Tel: 01225 477101
Website:
www.visitbath.co.uk

What's On

Look for *Venue, Bath Month* and *This Month in Bath* for details of what's on in Bath. The city's evening newspaper, *The Bath Chronicle*, provides listings too.

Visitor Call

Recorded information lines – calls cost 60p a minute:

Theatre information:
09068 360388
Exhibitions: 09068 360389
Guided walks:
09068 360393
Open-top bus tours:
09068 360394
Coach tours:
09068 360395
Boat trips: 09068 360396

Theatre Royal box office:
01225 448844

Guided walks

Bizarre Bath;
tel: 01225 335124
Ghost Walks of Bath;
tel: 01225 463618
Mayor of Bath's Corps of Honorary Guides;
tel: 01225 4777411
Jane Austen Walk;
tel: 01225 443000

TRAVEL
Airport

The nearest airport is Bristol International Airport.
Tel: 01275 474444

Bus information

Bath bus station is in Dorchester Street (map D6), opposite the railway station and a five-minute walk from the city centre.
Traveline: 0870 608 2608
Badgerline: 01225 464446

Shopmobility

4 Railway Street (map D6)
by Bath bus station
For the loan of manual or powered wheelchairs and electric scooters for those with limited mobility.
Tel: 01225 481744

Taxis

Ranks at Bath Spa station (map D6), Orange Grove (map D4), Milsom Street (map C3), New Orchard Street (map D5).

Train information

Bath Spa railway station is in Dorchester Street (map D6), just a five-minute walk from the city centre. There is a taxi rank and cycle racks outside the station and a cash dispensing machine inside.
Rail enquiries: 0845 7484950.

PARK AND RIDE
map: see page 100
The four park-and-ride services offer frequent non-stop buses to different locations in central Bath. They are:

Lansdown Park and Ride
Signposted from the A46/A420 junction, 3 miles south of the M4
Operates from 7.30–19.30 Mon–Fri.
No. 31 buses leave every 15 min for Queen Square.

Newbridge Park and Ride
On the A4 Upper Bristol Road
Operates from 7.30–19.30 Mon–Sat.
No. 21 bus leaves every 15 min Mon–Fri, and every 10 min Sat, to Westgate Buildings.

Odd Down Park and Ride
On the A367
Operates from 7.30–19.30 Mon–Sat.
No. 41 buses leave every 12 min to St James's Parade.

University Park and Ride
Signposted from the A36; at the University of Bath, Claverton Down on the A3062
Operates from 8.30–18.30 Sats only.
No. 19 bus departs every 15 min for Terrace Walk.

BANKS AND POST OFFICE
Cash dispensers
Bath Spa Station; map D6
Barclays, Manvers Street; map E5–E6
Lloyds TSB, Lower Borough Walls; map C5–D5
Lloyds TSB, Milsom Street; map C3
HSBC, Milsom Street; map C3
HSBC, Southgate; map D5
NatWest, High Street; map D4
Royal Bank of Scotland, Quiet Street; map C3
Lloyds TSB, Upper Borough Walls; map C4–D4

Main Post Office
New Bond Street; map D3

SPORT
Bath Sports and Leisure Centre:
01225 4622565
Bath Rugby Club:
09068 884554
Bath Racecourse:
01295 688030

EMERGENCIES
Fire, ambulance or police
Tel: 999

Bath Police Station
Manvers Street; map E6–E7
Tel: 01225 444343

Royal United Hospital
Combe Park (including accident and emergency)
Tel: 01225 428331

24-hour petrol station
Esso Filling Station, Churchill Bridge; map C6

Emergency breakdown
Bath Car Care Centre, Lower Bristol Road; map A6–C6
Tel: 01225 481920 or 07957 873283

INDEX

CITY-BREAK GUIDES

These full-colour guides come with stunning new photography capturing the special essence of some of Britain's loveliest cities. Each is divided into easy-reference sections where you will find something for everyone – from walk maps to fabulous shopping, from sightseeing highlights to keeping the kids entertained, from recommended restaurants to tours and trips ... and much, much more.

BATH
Stylish and sophisticated – just two adjectives that sum up the delightful Roman city of Bath, which saw a resurgence of popularity in Georgian times and in the 21st century is once again a vibrant and exciting place to be.

CAMBRIDGE
Historic architecture mingles with hi-tech revolution in the university city of Cambridge, where stunning skylines over surrounding fenland meet the style and sophistication of modern city living.

CHESTER
Savour the historic delights of the Roman walls and charming black-and-white architecture, blending seamlessly with the contemporary shopping experience that make Chester such an exhilarating city.

OXFORD

City and university life intertwine in Oxford, with its museums, bookstores and all manner of sophisticated entertainment to entice visitors to its hidden alleyways, splendid quadrangles and skyline of dreaming spires.

STRATFORD

Universally appealing, the picturesque streets of Stratford draw visitors back time and again to explore Shakespeare's birthplace, but also to relish the theatres and stylish riverside town that exists today.

YORK

A warm northern welcome and modern-day world-class shops and restaurants await you in York, along with its ancient city walls, Viking connections and magnificent medieval Minster rising above the rooftops.

Jarrold Publishing, Healey House, Dene Road, Andover, Hampshire, SP10 2AA, UK
Sales: 01264 409206
Enquiries: 01264 409200
Fax: 01264 334110
e-mail: heritagesales@jarrold-publishing.co.uk
website: www.britguides.com

MAIN ROUTES IN AND OUT OF BATH

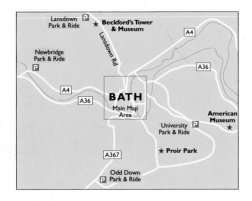

Park and ride services leave regularly for central Bath from:

Lansdown Park and Ride
Signposted from the A46/A420 junction,
3 miles south of the M4

Newbridge Park and Ride
On the A4 Upper Bristol Road

Odd Down Park and Ride
On the A367

University Park and Ride
Signposted from the A36; at the University of Bath,
Claverton Down on the A3062

See page 95 for further details